NEW DIRECTIONS FOR TEA

MW01041150

Marilla D. Svinicki, *University of Texas at Austin*
EDITOR-IN-CHIEF

R. Eugene Rice, *American Association for Higher Education*
CONSULTING EDITOR

Online Student Ratings of Instruction

D. Lynn Sorenson
Brigham Young University

Trav D. Johnson
Brigham Young University

EDITORS

Number 96, Winter 2003

JOSSEY-BASS
San Francisco

ONLINE STUDENT RATINGS OF INSTRUCTION
D. Lynn Sorenson, Trav D. Johnson (eds.)
New Directions for Teaching and Learning, no. 96
Marilla D. Svinicki, Editor-in-Chief
R. Eugene Rice, Consulting Editor

Microfilm copies of issues and articles are available in 16mm and 35mm, as well as microfiche in 105mm, through University Microfilms Inc., 300 North Zeeb Road, Ann Arbor, Michigan 48106-1346.

ISSN 0271-0633   electronic ISSN 1536-0768

NEW DIRECTIONS FOR TEACHING AND LEARNING is part of The Jossey-Bass Higher and Adult Education Series and is published quarterly by Wiley Subscription Services, Inc., A Wiley Company, at Jossey-Bass, 989 Market Street, San Francisco, California 94103-1741. Periodicals postage paid at San Francisco, California, and at additional mailing offices. Postmaster: Send address changes to New Directions for Teaching and Learning, Jossey-Bass, 989 Market Street, San Francisco, California 94103-1741.

New Directions for Teaching and Learning is indexed in College Student Personnel Abstracts, Contents Pages in Education, and Current Index to Journals in Education (ERIC).

SUBSCRIPTIONS cost $80 for individuals and $160 for institutions, agencies, and libraries. Prices subject to change.

EDITORIAL CORRESPONDENCE should be sent to the editor-in-chief, Marilla D. Svinicki, The Center for Teaching Effectiveness, University of Texas at Austin, Main Building 2200, Austin, TX 78712-1111.

Cover photograph by Richard Blair/Color & Light © 1990.

www.josseybass.com

CONTENTS

1. Charting the Uncharted Seas of Online Student Ratings of Instruction 1

D. Lynn Sorenson, Christian Reiner

Islands of online-rating systems are sprinkled across the globe. Separated by uncharted seas, most have arisen independently without the benefit of other innovators' "maps." In facilitating discussion among these "early adopters," the authors preview Web-based evaluation issues to provide a navigation tool for explorers of online student ratings.

2. Online Course Evaluation and Reporting in Higher Education 25

Kevin M. Hoffman

Results of a national survey indicate an increase in the use of the Internet for student ratings of instruction.

3. Online Ratings: Fact and Fiction 31

Nedra Hardy

Administrators, faculty, and students sometimes express reservations about online student ratings. At Northwestern University, ongoing research about online student evaluations has helped dispel some common (mis)perceptions.

4. Psychometric Properties of Student Ratings of Instruction in Online and On-Campus Courses 39

Debbie E. McGhee, Nana Lowell

To compare online and paper-based methods of student ratings of instruction, researchers examine mean ratings, inter-rater reliabilities, and factor structure of items.

5. Online Student Ratings: Will Students Respond? 49

Trav D. Johnson

Based on five years of research, a case study focuses on the response rates for one university's online evaluation system. The author identifies factors that influence response rates and suggests strategies to increase student participation.

6. Online Reporting of Results of Online Student Ratings 61

Donna C. Llewellyn

When examining the merits of online reporting of student-rating results, universities must consider security, logistics, confidentiality, and other important issues.

About This Publication. Since 1980, *New Directions for Teaching and Learning (NDTL)* has brought a unique blend of theory, research, and practice to leaders in postsecondary education. *NDTL* sourcebooks strive not only for solid substance but also for timeliness, compactness, and accessibility.

The series has four goals: to inform readers about current and future directions in teaching and learning in postsecondary education, to illuminate the context that shapes these new directions, to illustrate these new directions through examples from real settings, and to propose ways in which these new directions can be incorporated into still other settings.

This publication reflects the view that teaching deserves respect as a high form of scholarship. We believe that significant scholarship is conducted not only by researchers who report results of empirical investigations but also by practitioners who share disciplined reflections about teaching. Contributors to *NDTL* approach questions of teaching and learning as seriously as they approach substantive questions in their own disciplines, and they deal not only with pedagogical issues but also with the intellectual and social context in which these issues arise. Authors deal on the one hand with theory and research and on the other with practice, and they translate from research and theory to practice and back again.

About This Volume. Technology is having an impact on every aspect of higher education, from class management to grade delivery to student-faculty interactions. Each of these uses has its pluses and minuses, its critics and supporters. It is not surprising to find technology being explored as the answer to some of the problems of students' evaluation of teaching. This issue of *NDTL* tackles that very question and, as with most examinations of technology, finds that the answers are not simple—but they are encouraging.

Marilla D. Svinicki
Editor-in-Chief

MARILLA D. SVINICKI is director of the Center for Teaching Effectiveness at the University of Texas at Austin.

Are online student ratings the "wave of the future"? This chapter introduces numerous advantages and challenges of adopting an online system for student evaluation of teaching; in it, the authors preview the research of the other authors of this volume and suggest areas that universities can investigate when determining the desirability of initiating an online ratings system for student evaluation of instruction.

Charting the Uncharted Seas of Online Student Ratings of Instruction

D. Lynn Sorenson, Christian Reiner

In attempting to "chart uncharted seas," it is sometimes helpful to look back at earlier journeys that were once uncharted but are now well traveled. Consider that, in the 1970s, it seemed unlikely that word processing would be useful anywhere except in a typing pool. Now it is ubiquitous, and typing pools, as such, have ceased to exist. Then, in the 1980s, when the Internet made its arcane and awkward entrance onto the world's stage, it appeared to be a fun toy for playful "techies" or, perhaps, a serious communication device for NASA scientists. It seemed unlikely that it would affect much of anything in the real world or in most of academe. Now, time has revealed its irreplaceable value to all of academe, to business, to government, and even to isolated villagers in newly named countries. In a word, the world will never be the same.

Today nearly every function in society can be—and *is*—performed online: online shopping, online reservations, online chat rooms, online music, online movies, online dating, online counseling, online birthing instruction, and online funeral planning. And, of course, academe has embraced the Web for a myriad of functions: online admissions, online registration, online grades, online libraries, online databases, online research, online teaching, online testing, online conferences, and online universities! Is it such a far reach to imagine the Internet supplanting cumbersome paper systems for the student ratings of instruction in higher education—slowly now at first, and rapidly, even completely, in the future? Will paper ratings go the way of typing pools and slide rules?

The idea of an online student-rating system is a "cutting-edge" proposition (in comparison to a traditional paper-based system). An electronic system can provide nearly instantaneous recording of data, reduced processing time and costs, more accurate data collection and reporting, easy administration, faster completion for students, and longer, more thoughtful student comments. Dozens of colleges and universities have initiated online ratings of instruction for face-to-face classes—usually creating the systems in isolation, as "islands" unto themselves. Often they have been unaware of "neighboring islands" engaged in the same intense work of developing an online rating system. This volume endeavors to initiate communication and exchange among some "early adopters" in the United States and Australia. Who are the early adopters? How many institutions of higher education have implemented online student ratings of instruction?

Institutions Using Online Student Ratings

Until the publication of this volume, the study reported by Hmieleski and Champagne (2000) stood as the only available data on the number of institutions using online student evaluations. At that time, they found a meager 2 percent of the surveyed U.S. institutions reporting the campuswide use of online student ratings of instruction. As might be expected, many more institutions evaluate online courses through the Web now.

Current Survey Research. Kevin M. Hoffman (Chapter Two in this volume) provides more recent data about the pervasiveness of online ratings through 2002. Of the hundreds of campuses he surveyed, 17 percent of the responding institutions "reported using the Internet in some capacity to collect student evaluation data for face-to-face courses." Another "10 percent indicated that their institutions planned to initiate Internet evaluations of face-to-face courses in 2003." Still another 18 percent reported that their institutions were "in the process of reviewing Internet options." In other words, nearly half of the institutions responding to Hoffman's survey had initiated some degree of online ratings collection or were considering doing so.

Internet Resources. In an informal search of the World Wide Web in the summer of 2003, Susan J. Clark of Brigham Young University found some three dozen university Web sites with information about their institutions' use of online student ratings to evaluate face-to-face classes, either for entire campuses or for entire divisions, colleges, schools, or departments (see the Appendix at the end of this chapter). An additional twenty-five institutions' Web sites indicated that their campuses were using online ratings solely for online courses. The number of postsecondary education institutions implementing online student ratings is growing. (For updated information on institutions using online student ratings or to share information about an institution's use of online student ratings, go to the Web site for Online Student Evaluation of Teaching (OnSET), http://OnSET. byu.edu.)

This volume can serve as a guidebook for travelers exploring these "islands" of online ratings "sprinkled across the globe." Riding a wave of the future, the authors have braved uncharted seas to research and create systems where the Internet pervades the process of student evaluation of instruction.

Other travelers who wish to explore these islands of innovation must engage in some important preparation before embarking on the journey. That is, they must first contextualize online ratings within the framework of student evaluation of instruction, in general, and then within the even larger context of the teaching-evaluation process in higher education.

Context

Student evaluations of teaching began in the fifties and sixties. Through the years, they have been driven by many factors: accountability, teaching improvement, legal considerations, and budget concerns, to name a few (Ory, 2000). Student ratings of instruction are "arguably the largest single area of research in postsecondary education" (Theall and Franklin, 1990). In 1996, researchers at the University of Michigan estimated that more than two thousand articles about student ratings of instruction had been printed over the previous fifty years (McKeachie and Kaplan, 1996).

This intense scrutiny, research, and publication have continued; for example, *New Directions for Teaching and Learning (NDTL)* has published three volumes related to the evaluation of teaching within a recent two-year period: *Evaluating Teaching in Higher Education: A Vision for the Future* (K. E. Ryan, editor, 2000); *Fresh Approaches to the Evaluation of Teaching* (C. Knapper and P. Cranton, editors, 2001); and *Techniques and Strategies for Interpreting Student Evaluations* (K. G. Lewis, editor, 2001). An earlier *NDTL* can serve as an excellent resource: *Student Ratings of Instruction: Issues for Improving Practice* (M. Theall and J. Franklin, editors, 1990). In addition, *New Directions for Institutional Research* issued another important resource, *The Student Ratings Debate: Are They Valid? How Can We Best Use Them?* (M. Theall, P. C. Abrami, and L. A. Mets, editors, 2001). All of these New Directions publications provide excellent resources for academics and administrators to review the important contextual issues of teaching evaluation and improvement (of which online ratings of instruction have become a part).

Michael Theall, respected researcher, practitioner, and author on the evaluation of teaching, has suggested a context for good practice in teaching evaluation (regardless of whether ratings are collected online or on paper). In addition to emphasizing that student ratings are an important part of evaluation, Theall (2002) suggests a number of guidelines for an effective teaching evaluation process and system:

- Establish the purposes of the evaluation and who the users will be.
- Include stakeholders in decisions about evaluation process and policy.
- Keep in mind a balance between individual and institutional needs.

- Publicly present clear information about the evaluation criteria, process, and procedures.
- Be sure to provide resources for improvement and support of teaching and teachers.
- Build a coherent system for evaluation, rather than a piecemeal process.
- Establish clear lines of responsibility and reporting for those who administer the system.
- Invest in the superior evaluation system and evaluate it regularly.
- Use, adapt, or develop instruments suited to institutional and individual needs.
- Use multiple sources of information for evaluation decisions.
- Collect data on ratings and validate the instrument(s) used.
- Produce reports that can be easily and accurately understood.
- Educate the users of rating results to avoid misuse and misinterpretation.
- Keep formative evaluation confidential and separate from summative decision making.
- In summative decisions, compare teachers on the basis of data from similar teaching situations.
- Consider the appropriate use of evaluation data for assessment and other purposes.
- Seek expert outside assistance when necessary or appropriate.

(See the Web site http://www.byu.edu/fc/pages/tchlrnpages/focusnews letters/Focus_Fall_2002.pdf.)

As the possibility of Web-based ratings has arisen within this context of teaching evaluation, some innovators have sought wider support for new online student evaluation systems. Given that the initiation of an online ratings system is a sizable endeavor—involving seemingly "a cast of thousands" and substantial resources—why would any institution want to sail into this "uncharted sea"?

Why Consider an Online Student Ratings System?

A closer look at some of the possible advantages of an online rating system is helpful to understand why colleges are considering and initiating the use of the Internet as an alternative to the traditional paper-pencil rating medium. This discussion about advantages of online course ratings necessarily involves a comparison of online and paper-pencil rating systems because the online ratings usually replace or supplement paper ratings.

Time. An online course-rating system frees up valuable class time because students can complete their ratings outside of class. Not only teachers value this advantage, but several studies have shown that students also tend to perceive saved class time as an advantage (Dommeyer, Baum, and Hanna, 2002; Johnson, 2001; Layne, DeCristoforo, and McGinty, 1999). In

Chapter Seven of this volume, Timothy Bothell and Tom Henderson discuss, among other things, the use of class time for student ratings.

The class-time-saving advantages of online ratings come with some possible problems. Some students are concerned that they and their peers may be less likely to complete their course ratings if they must do them outside of class in their free time, rather than doing them in class (Hardy, 2002; Johnson, 2001; Layne, DeCristoforo, and McGinty, 1999). In Chapter Five of this volume, Trav Johnson reports some student concerns and suggestions on this topic.

Besides freeing up valuable class time, online course ratings provide students with a longer time period during which to complete their ratings. When filling out forms in class, students must do so in a few minutes. Using an online student-rating system increases this time span because ratings are completed outside of class. Because students have more time to complete their course ratings, the quantity and quality of their written responses may increase. When completing online ratings, students' comments may be longer and more thoughtful because they are more likely to provide their feedback when they feel ready to do so and with sufficient time to write all they want to write. Some research has shown that students completing online ratings tend to provide more and longer written comments than students using the traditional paper-pencil process.In Chapter Three of this volume, Nedra Hardy compares students' written comments collected through each medium. In addition, Trav Johnson addresses this issue in Chapter Five of this volume.

An online course-rating system also improves on one of the major weaknesses of paper-pencil course ratings—high turnaround time (that is, the time required for instructors to receive reports of results after students have submitted their ratings). Of the 105 colleges responding to Hmieleski's previously mentioned survey (2000), 65 percent reported that, on average, it takes three weeks to two months before teachers receive the results of their course ratings. An online ratings system can substantially shorten the time to receive ratings reports, thereby enabling teachers to consider and act on student feedback in a more timely manner.

The administration of course ratings is eased considerably by an online system. An automated Web-based system saves much of the time spent on printing and distributing the rating forms, cleaning up the returned forms and running them through a scanner, and distributing the results. Moreover, the use of an online rating system frees up time for department secretaries and others who currently spend hours transcribing handwritten student feedback to ensure students' anonymity.

Flexibility. In some online rating systems, instructors are given the flexibility to adapt and personalize the rating forms. They can easily change or add questions (or both) to elicit feedback according to their individual needs. Of course, most institutions with online rating systems do not allow unlimited "teacher tinkering" with the form. The system has to ensure that the mandated items cannot be changed or eliminated by instructors.

Another benefit of the online system is the flexibility it provides in accessing reports. In most cases, as long as instructors have access to computers and the Internet, they can look at and print their online rating results at their own convenience.

In addition to having personalized rating forms and the ease of accessing reports, teachers can use an online system to obtain midterm and ongoing feedback from students in addition to the required end-of-course ratings. In a study of an online rating system that allowed for ongoing feedback, students indicated that they liked the availability of such a system even if they did not take advantage of it often. To them, it was good to know that they could give feedback if they desired (Ravelli, 2000). The Curtin University School of Physiotherapy has developed a comprehensive system for online feedback, reported in Chapter Eight of this volume by Beatrice Tucker, Sue Jones, Leon Straker, and Joan Cole. In addition, Cheryl Davis Bullock outlines a mid-course online evaluation system in Chapter Nine of this volume. As mentioned earlier in the "Time" section of this chapter, an asset of the online systems is the flexibility afforded to student respondents when completing their course ratings. With the online systems, students gain flexibility as to when and where they complete the rating form, provided they have access to a computer and the Internet. Enabling students to complete the form at their own convenience increases the likelihood that responding students will have the time needed to consider their rating and write all that they want to say in the student comments section.

Quantity and Quality of Written Comments. Research indicates that students provide more and longer responses online than they do using a traditional paper-pencil system (Hardy, 2002; Hmieleski and Champagne, 2000; Johnson, 2001; Layne, DeCristoforo, and McGinty, 1999). The greater length and frequency of written responses may be due to students being less rushed in giving feedback, students feeling that typing their responses is easier and faster than writing them, and students now believing that their handwriting cannot be used to identify them (Johnson, 2001; Layne, DeCristoforo, and McGinty, 1999). Students have also reported that online course ratings allow them more time to consider their answers and provide more thoughtful written responses (Johnson, 2001; Ravelli, 2000; see also Hardy, Chapter Three, and Johnson, Chapter Five in this volume, for their studies about students' written comments).

Reporting. Having used online course ratings for several years now, the Georgia Institute of Technology has experienced several benefits from the electronic reporting of course-rating results. Specialized reports are fairly easy to create and make available to all users; reports can be accessed from a personal computer; the rating results are more accessible to a broader group of individuals (for example, researchers); data are more readily available for analysis across different types of classes and different course sections; and perhaps most important, reports are available almost immediately

(Llewellyn, 2002; Donna C. Llewellyn amplifies and updates these earlier studies in Chapter Six of this volume).

The crucial difference between Web-based evaluation reporting systems and paper evaluation reporting systems appears to be in the time it takes to get the data into the system for the processing of the results. When the data obtained by a paper-pencil system are entered into an electronic system, the same reporting benefits could be realized as those experienced by the Georgia Institute of Technology for the reporting of online ratings. Still, online course ratings have an edge on paper-pencil ratings in regard to turn-around time because of the reduced time needed to collect and enter data in the paper-pencil system.

Costs. Online student-rating systems are generally perceived as less expensive than paper-pencil rating systems. Automating the course-rating process eliminates the paper costs and reduces personnel costs for processing rating forms. Human involvement in the process of collecting, entering, and reporting course-rating data is minimized. One study suggests that conducting course ratings online leads to savings of 97 percent over the traditional paper-pencil method (see Hmieleski and Champagne, 2000). However, Theall (2000) has questioned the generalizability of this study because it "present[ed] the best case for electronic data processing and the worst case for paper-based systems." Bothell and Henderson (Chapter Seven in this volume) have undertaken a more rigorous costs study. They found the overall costs for online systems substantially lower than those for paper-based systems.

Challenges for Online Course Ratings

Online student evaluations of teaching present a number of challenges. Some difficulties are overstated during early preconception (or misperception) stages; others are unforeseen until the implementation (or maintenance) stages. This section outlines some of the common challenges of online student-rating systems.

Response Rates. Response rates are one of the most frequently raised issues in discussions of online student ratings of instruction; they are also becoming the area most often studied (for example, Cummings, Ballantyne, and Fowler, 2001; Dommeyer, Baum, and Hanna, 2002; Hmieleski, 2000; Johnson, 2002; Hardy, 2002; McGourty, Scoles, and Thorpe, 2002a). Some Web-based ratings have yielded lower response rates than paper-based systems. Researchers have suggested possible explanations for the lower response rates: perceived lack of anonymity of responses, lack of compulsion to complete ratings online, student apathy, inconvenience, technical problems, and required time for completing the ratings (Ballantyne, 2000; Dommeyer, Baum, and Hanna, 2002).

Several studies have shown that it is possible to spur response rates and even to obtain response rates of 80 percent and higher (Cummings,

Ballantyne, and Fowler, 2001; Goodman and Campbell, 1999; Ha and Marsh, n.d.; Hardy, 2002; Hmieleski, 2000; Johnson, 2002; McGourty, Scoles, and Thorpe, 2002a). In Chapter Ten of this volume, Christina Ballantyne elaborates on these issues; see also Hardy, Chapter Three, and Johnson, Chapter Five.

Response Biases. Some faculty are also concerned about response bias, which they perceive as linked to response rates. They wonder to what degree the group of responding students is representative of the whole class and to what degree the results are generalizable. For example, some studies have shown that students with higher grade-point averages (GPAs) tend to be more likely to complete online student ratings than students with lower GPAs (Layne, DeCristoforo, and McGinty, 1999; McGourty, Scoles, and Thorpe, 2002a). Researchers who have also studied a number of student-rating biases have found mixed or inconclusive results: gender biases (Dommeyer, Baum, and Hanna, 2002; Layne, DeCristoforo, and McGinty, 1999); year-in-school biases (Layne, DeCristoforo, and McGinty, 1999; McGourty, Scoles, and Thorpe, 2002a); and department, discipline, or course biases (Goodman and Campbell, 1999; Layne, DeCristoforo, and McGinty, 1999; Thorpe, 2002). More research on response bias—especially in regard to online student ratings of instruction—is needed to determine if, how, and to what degree online student ratings may favor responses from certain groups of students.

Instructors are also concerned that a low response rate for online ratings might bias written responses. Some worry that written comments may be predominantly negative because students with low opinions of the course and instructor might be more likely to respond than students with high opinions. Hardy's study at Northwestern University (Chapter Three in this volume) showed no predominance of negative comments in online ratings compared with those found in paper-pencil ratings.

Comparability. Faculty are understandably apprehensive about student ratings of instruction because student evaluations—whether paper or Web based—are usually an important measurement used to make personnel decisions. Are results of Web-based ratings and paper-based ratings comparable? Studies so far have suggested no consistent differences; results are essentially the same overall, even though some variation exists from study to study (Hardy, 2002; Johnson, 2002; and Thorpe, 2002). For more recent research and syntheses on this subject, see Chapter Four in this volume by Debbie E. McGhee and Nana Lowell; see also Chapters Three, Four, and Five in this volume.

Dependence on Technology. Reliance on technology can adversely affect accessibility to an online course-rating system in several ways. Low levels of computer literacy may exclude certain students from submitting their ratings online (Cummings, Ballantyne, and Fowler, 2001). Likewise, computer problems can prevent students from submitting their ratings online (Dommeyer, Baum, and Hanna, 2002). In addition, students who do not have easy access to computers may decide not to submit their ratings.

Using computers in a laboratory may be inconvenient for some students because the computers may be slow (Ravelli, 2000) or because they have to wait in line to get access to the computers.

Problems with technology can detract from the advantages of online course ratings in at least two ways. First, these problems may adversely affect the attitude of potential users and diminish their willingness to use an online evaluation system. Moreover, the group of students entering their course ratings online may be biased because certain students are either excluded from responding or may choose not to respond due to accessibility problems. This is a particularly important issue for disabled student participants. A school that is relying solely on the Internet for collecting student ratings (and reporting results) must account for technology-related accessibility issues. Failure to do so will raise issues of fairness, reliability, validity, and access—and may cause legal liability problems.

Convenience Versus Inconvenience. Because of its adaptability and accessibility, an online course-rating system can meet the various needs of students, teachers, and administrators. However, a study at California State University–Northridge suggested that convenience is not an inherent part of an online rating system (Dommeyer, Baum, and Hanna, 2002). In this study, students reported that it took too much time to complete the ratings online, that the log-on process was complicated, and that they had computer problems. Apparently online systems need to be designed and implemented thoughtfully and with care to fully tap into their potential advantage of convenience.

The feedback from students using an online system can prove crucial for achieving success. Among other things, studies so far have shown that students value an online evaluation tool that is readily accessed and easy to understand and use (Layne, DeCristoforo, and McGinty, 1999; Ravelli, 2000). If students have to wait in line in a computer lab to fill out their rating forms, if they run into computer problems when filling out or submitting the form, or if they have a hard time navigating the system, they will be less likely to complete Web-based ratings.

Initiating, Developing, and Financing an Online System. Transitioning from paper-pencil student ratings to online ratings requires a substantial initial investment of resources. Resources spent in this way obviously cannot be spent for other purposes. This can be problematic considering the tight budgets within which many schools operate today. When calculating the initial set-up costs, it is important to consider that purchasing a student-rating system may be cheaper than developing a new one (Ha and Marsh, n.d.). In Bothell and Henderson's study (Chapter Seven) of the costs of paper versus online student-ratings systems, they report that, overall, an online system costs less. But when transitioning from an established paper system (where development costs are already largely met) to an online system, the initial out-of-pocket costs to develop the online system are substantial. On the other hand, on many campuses where old paper-based systems (and their equipment) have become outdated and obsolete, the need arises to invest in a new system, whether paper based or online. Individual campuses must appraise the needs of their own campuses as they arrive at these junctures.

Anonymity and Confidentiality. Students seem to have dual perceptions about the anonymity of ratings they submit online. These differing student interpretations may suggest reasons for the discrepancies in the results of studies about some students' views: some students view paper-pencil ratings as being more confidential than online ratings, whereas others believe online ratings are more confidential. On the one hand, some wonder if the origin of their online comments remains confidential because they have to identify themselves when logging into the system (Dommeyer, Baum, and Hanna, 2002; Hardy, 2002; Layne, DeCristoforo, and McGinty, 1999). On the other hand, some perceive anonymity as an advantage of an online rating system because their handwriting cannot be used to identify them (Ballantyne, 2000; Dommeyer, Baum, and Hanna, 2002; Layne, DeCristoforo, and McGinty, 1999).

To help ensure confidentiality, student comments can be separated from student identifiers after the data have been entered into the system (McGourty, Scoles, and Thorpe, 2002a). However, simply designing an online rating system to ensure confidentiality is not sufficient to resolve some students' concerns about the confidentiality of their online responses. Students also need to be educated, assured, and reassured concerning the system's ability to guarantee the confidentiality of their responses (Goodman and Campbell, 1999; Layne, DeCristoforo, and McGinty, 1999).

Data Access. Online rating systems allow the storage and use of data in such a way that it will be more easily accessible to a broader, but still appropriate, group of people for various purposes. This raises the question of who should have access to the data (Llewellyn, 2002). Researchers are among those who have marked interest in the data generated by online ratings systems. If and when they have access to these data, at what point do students "start to become subjects of human research" (Zimitat and Crebert, 2002)? In addition to researchers, who besides the instructors whose courses were rated online should have access to these data—chairs, deans, students, the public? Several chapters in this volume address this question; see, for example, Llewellyn, Chapter Six.

Control. As students complete their ratings outside of class, much less control can be exerted over the conditions under which they do so. Some teachers express concern that students may be influenced by peer pressure if they discuss their ratings with others before filling out their forms. Others are concerned that students who are registered for a class can fill out the rating form online even if they never attended class (Ha and Marsh, n.d.).

Culture Change. Colleges that intend to replace paper-pencil course ratings with online ratings face the challenge of changing a well-established customary practice. As Machiavelli observed more than five hundred years ago, "nothing is more difficult to handle, more doubtful of success, nor more dangerous to manage, than to put oneself at the head of introducing new orders" (Machiavelli, 1513). Online-ratings innovators need to understand and effectively deal with the possible reasons for, and expressions of, resistance among the stakeholders affected by the change. To address some of these difficulties and resistance to "new orders," consider the organizational issues and suggestions addressed below.

Organizational Issues and Suggestions

Proposing a change in student evaluations of instruction affects almost every unit and every person in the campus community. Faculty are the most affected by this change; in fact, the effect on them is cumulative, if it is considered that most evaluation systems stay in place for many years. Consequently, faculty are usually the most anxious about evaluation and the most resistant to a change in the system. Faculty resistance to changes in the design of the survey, in the frequency of its administration, and in its medium of administration—from paper to online—is hardly based on faculty affection for the old paper system. Rather, their resistance often seems based more on their preconceived notions about the new system and their lingering doubts about the older system (see Hardy, Chapter Three, for more about faculty preconceptions).

The experience of institutions initiating online evaluations suggests that a campus considering *any* change in the student ratings—whether it be going online, changing the items, shortening or lengthening the survey, changing the evaluation from optional to mandatory, or requiring it more often—had better be prepared to justify the larger concept of evaluation of teaching, the specific process of students rating their instruction, and even the idea that there is such a thing as "good teaching" that can promote "good learning." The previously mentioned *NDTL* volumes serve this purpose well. In addition, William Cashin has created a valuable, short monograph called "Student Ratings of Teaching: The Research Revisited" (IDEA Paper No. 32, 1995). This eight-page review of the literature on student ratings was a useful resource in re-educating the BYU community about the relevant research and the value of student ratings. An additional six IDEA Papers address student ratings and faculty evaluation; these monographs are available on the IDEA Center Web site at http://www.idea.ksu.edu/papers.

Organizational Change Theory. A brief look at organizational theory—especially change theory and practice—is appropriate at this point. Beckhard and Harris (1977) proposed a plan for managing the politics of a transition; they suggested the following steps for securing the support of important stakeholders:

1. Identify target individuals and groups whose commitment is needed.
2. Define the critical mass needed to ensure the effective implementation.
3. Develop a plan for getting the commitment from the critical mass.
4. Develop a monitoring system to assess progress.

Tichy and Sherman also provide a model for moving ahead with an initiative, incorporating the political "buy-in" above. They suggest three stages in the innovation process: awakening, envisioning, and rearchitecting (1994). For a closer look at these processes, see Tichy's useful short "Handbook for Revolutionaries" (1983, pp. 365–448). These organizational studies and "best practices" are based on business models, but their ideas have near-universal applicability for universities and other organizations.

For decades, organizational scholar David A. Whetten has researched organizational behavior and change. He has found that it is not uncommon for those leading an organization and those leading a particular change in that organization to have differences of opinion about the meaning and merit of concerns expressed by those affected by the change. From their perspective, university administrators might be inclined to assume that there is such a thing as a perfect plan for change—hence, zero objections to a planned change constitutes a "perfect score" for the plan, the planners, or both. Obviously, this expectation is unrealistic. Planners cannot control all the factors that affect how organization members will respond to an organizational change. Nor is it a measurable standard; it is difficult to distinguish between resistance to the proposal and strongly worded suggestions for making the proposal better.

For example, university planners excited about an innovation may be tempted to discount *any* opposition. They may be inclined to believe that people inherently resist change in their routine, and therefore assume that all organizational changes will provoke knee-jerk objections. Moreover, the change agents may be so enthralled with their plan that they cannot conceive of any legitimate objection. Regardless, if the change agents "cut corners"—leaving out important stakeholders, disallowing opportunities for feedback, or discounting legitimate objections—the advocates will be short-changing the stakeholders and themselves by not allowing opportunity for legitimate objections to a proposed plan.

Because student ratings are central to the evaluation of faculty and the overall performance of a university's teaching mission, changes in the student evaluation process are, indeed, likely to provoke strong objections. Hence, it is important that those involved in the planning of changes to the student-rating system are aware of the types of objections they are likely to encounter. In fact, many objections can be anticipated and countered through effective planning and execution of the change plan (Whetten, personal communication, Aug. 2003).

Recognizing Types of Objections. Whetten suggests two types of objections to change (in a student ratings system) that are likely to arise. Those affected by the proposed change are likely to express concerns about the specific proposed change in the student-rating system (for example, "Putting student ratings online will likely decrease the response rate"), or the legitimacy of the student evaluation itself (for example, "Student ratings are inherently biased").

The first type of objection comes from "experts"—those who believe they have an informed opinion about the changes. The second type of objection typically comes from "critics"—those who have a vested interest in making student ratings "just go away." To gain the support of experts, they need to be convinced that the proposal is sound and that the implementation plan is well conceived. Critics capitalize on the lack of agreement among the experts to challenge the legitimacy of the activity with statements like, "If we can't agree on the 'right way' to do this, then why are we doing student ratings at all?" (Whetten, personal communication, Aug. 2003)

By understanding the types of objections likely to arise, planners can first anticipate and then prepare for both kinds of objections.Ultimately they can use the proposed change in student ratings as an opportunity to reinforce the value of student feedback (Theall and Franklin, 1990), the importance of the evaluation of instruction (Cashin, 1995; Braskamp and Ory, 1994), and the significance of learner-centered education (Fink, 2003; Weimer, 2002). By equipping themselves with knowledge and resources about student ratings of instruction and faculty evaluation, change agents are better able to develop an effective evaluations system and to promote it successfully to their colleagues.

As an aside, planners should not assume that they will always be able to recognize the "real" reasons behind a stated objection. Rarely do those raising objections state their assumptions or their motives—sometimes because they are unknowable: "I don't know why I don't like this, but I just know I don't like it." At Brigham Young University, some faculty who had traditionally resented the old paper-based ratings—and had achieved only a wary tolerance of them in the past—found their earlier mistrust of student ratings reemerging when changes in the student evaluation system were proposed. Whetten offers this advice for addressing these kinds of attitudes: Do not waste time trying to ferret out a person's motives because they are often buried or even unknowable. Take objections at face value, but also do not assume that every objection can be satisfied with a reasonable answer (Whetten, personal communication, Aug. 2003).

Anticipating Targets of Objections. "[K]ey dimensions of resistance [to change] are power, fear, and imposition of the will of others" (O'Toole 1995, p. 239). Whetten notes that research on organizational change suggests that affected individuals are most likely to resist changes that are perceived to be unnecessary (for example, proposed change not needed or too costly), or flawed (for example, good idea but poor execution or implementation). What people predictably object to is imposed changes (things they do not initiate) that are disruptive ("I can't get my work done") and arguably unnecessary ("Things are just fine the way they are"). Advocates for a change from paper-based student evaluations to online evaluations—or advocates for *any* organizational change—should be prepared to address issues and answer questions raised about the proposed changes in a number of ways.

Unnecessary Change (Why Change?)

Why do we need to change (to solve a problem, exploit an opportunity, reach a goal, and so forth)?

What or who will benefit? What are the benefits to faculty? To students? To the institution? How will this change help us better accomplish our mission?

Who will bear the costs? What is the cost-benefit ratio? Are the proposed benefits worth the "wear and tear" on the organization and its members?

Flawed Plan or Process (What, How, and When to Change?)

Is the scope of the proposal about right (or too big or too small)?

Are the choices or the planning well informed? (Who decided to change? What information was used? Who was consulted?)

Is the decision process fair and transparent (important stakeholders included, credible representatives selected, periodic progress reports made, a period provided for comment on draft proposals, and so forth)?

(Whetten, personal communication, Aug. 2003)

Often a change in one aspect of the student rating process has a "flypaper" effect; it attracts ideas to change related features and functions. At BYU, the innovation of online ratings was made more complicated by the fact that the university administration mandated that a new survey instrument be designed, that a new data-gathering process be initiated (on the Web), and that a new rate of frequency be required (that is, every class, every semester, every teacher, and every student). In other words, both the instrument and the medium were to be changed. Hence, the content, the medium, and the frequency were *all* undergoing transformation at the same time.

Any change requires strategic planning, and one this all-encompassing requires a myriad of strategies about the "process" of the change. Burke (2002) describes *process* as "how the change[s are] planned, launched, or fully implemented, and once into implementation, sustained" (p. 14). At BYU this process has taken the better part of a decade. With the upper administration exerting pressure to initiate the new system(s), many of the procedures were created by lower-level administrators "just in time." Most BYU faculty and administrators supported the changes, but those who did not were vocal, visible, and visceral. Nevertheless, BYU's development of, and transition to, the online rating system has been a relatively successful process.

Implications, Ideas, and Suggestions for Preempting Legitimate Objections. To facilitate an effective change process, planners must be prepared to answer objections. Whetten offers several suggestions that may be helpful for those considering an organizational change such as initiating Web-based student evaluations.

To avoid the perception (or reality!) of a flawed plan (or process), make sure important stakeholders' views are incorporated into the decision-making process. Make the process transparent (publish periodic reports, make interim reports to the faculty senate, and so forth). If people feel that a process is well informed and fair, they are more likely to accept that the option they preferred was not chosen.

Carefully consider the tradeoff between size, speed, and scope of the innovation; that is, should the changes be made all at once ("Get it over with") or spread out over time ("Prolong the pain")? If it is likely that a proposed change will be perceived as excessive (in terms of size, speed, or scope), justify why this exception to normal, reasonable practice is required.

In addressing the cost-benefit ratio, acknowledge that any change (no matter how large or how often) is costly in terms of financial and other resources. Stipulate what can be done to minimize the costs and express appreciation to those who bear these costs.

To answer questions about the necessity of a change, advocates should not assume that just because they believe that a balanced scale is infinitely superior to an unbalanced scale (or whatever) that others will also believe this and take its assumed merits for granted. Make "nested explanations" available: a paragraph for the casual observer and a detailed report for the expert (Whetten, personal communication, 2003).

Hindsight suggests that "getting *all* the ducks lined up in advance"at BYU would have been impossible. ("Turning the Titanic," "herding cats," and other metaphors come to mind.) Nevertheless, accomplishing any such far-reaching change as a new evaluation system requires considerable planning, collaboration, and consulting. Stakeholders' buy-in cannot be overestimated, but this buy-in does not need to include every single stakeholder or every single faculty member. Isolated pockets of negativity should not be enough to sink a well-designed plan.

A word of advice is offered here about committees, task forces, and other groups involved in planning a change to the student evaluation system. Respected, knowledgeable stakeholders—who are mostly "on board" and known as persons who work in a timely manner to accomplish important goals—make the best members of groups researching possibilities and planning changes. Then, after the committees or task forces have made suggestions, ideas, and proposals, the content and process can be opened up to the faculty senate, technology council, student leadership association, and other groups for feedback, suggestions, and alternative options. At this point, the planners or originators need to fan out across campus—in person or online—to answer questions and gather feedback to improve the plan(s). As more supporters emerge, they can help "carry the ball" to, and for, their colleagues.

All discussions of online-rating collection return to issues of student evaluation of instruction and faculty evaluation in general. These "big-picture" issues are at the heart of an effective system for the evaluation of instruction and instructors. Within this context, what are some of the other important questions to ask as the process of considering online student ratings begins?

Usually discussion begins with one or more of these questions: "For what reasons might we consider converting our paper-based student rating system to an online system," and "Does our current student ratings instrument need to be changed, updated, or improved?" If so, should it be put online? How long has it been since the form was changed? On many campuses where the student rating system was developed in the seventies or eighties, new research about teaching and learning needs to be incorporated into a new, more effective instrument. At these same campuses, processing equipment has become outdated and obsolete. Some kind of change must happen soon to update these systems. Is it also time to consider converting to online evaluation, as Georgia Institute of Technology did in 1999 (see Chapter Four of this volume).

Assess Readiness. To initiate the change to an online system of course ratings, it is important to assess the readiness of the various stakeholders. Three main groups of stakeholders exist for student feedback systems—students, teachers, and survey administration staff (Ballantyne, 2000). It is important to assess their level of access to computer technology, their level of computer literacy, and their willingness to accept using an online system for student feedback (Cummings, Ballantyne, and Fowler, 2001). The purpose of the assessment is to make sure that the stakeholders are able and willing to use the system (see Chapter Ten in this volume). Readiness may be increased by answering objections early in the process.

Not only do the stakeholders need to be ready to use a Web-based system, but institutions intending to use online course ratings also need to make sure that their institutional technology system is ready to accommodate the use of online course ratings. This includes having adequate human and financial resources to implement and maintain the system and making sure that the system is adequately suited to meet the requirements for obtaining student feedback online (Ha and Marsh, n.d.).

Consider Unique Campus Situations. As campuses learn from and with each other about "best practices" in online student rating systems, they need to keep in mind that circumstances and needs vary from campus to campus. For some campuses, it may be easier to implement an online course-rating system than for others because of their existing technological infrastructure. Campuses may also vary in their budgets and in the levels of computer literacy of their students. Moreover, campuses that offer distance-education courses may have a special interest in online course rating because they can eliminate the time and costs required to mail rating forms. Based on these and other factors, campuses will vary in their approaches to the implementation of an online rating system. For example, BYU initiated its system campuswide at the behest of upper administration. On the other hand, Purdue University's online ratings were initiated by faculty in individual engineering schools—and were used *only* by those schools.

Educate Participants. The best online student-rating system would be of no use if stakeholders did not know how to use it. Educating stakeholders to use the system may involve training faculty about why and how to use the online rating system (McGourty, Scoles, and Thorpe, 2002b) and faculty demonstrating to students how to use the online system (Dommeyer, Baum, and Hanna, 2002)—or vice versa. Moreover, students need to know not only how to use the system but also that teachers pay attention to student feedback (Ballantyne, 2000; Cummings, Ballantyne, and Fowler, 2001; Johnson, 2002; Ravelli, 2000).

Promote Collaboration and Ownership. Yale and Columbia Universities have reached response rates of 85 percent and higher for Web-based ratings. Among other things, some institutions with high response rates appear to be involving faculty and students in ways that they feel ownership in the system.

At Columbia, faculty can provide input concerning the design and future features of the system. Some 20 percent of Columbia teachers are already using the online system either to customize their feedback forms or to obtain more feedback than solely the mandatory course ratings. Moreover, Columbia University has a system in place that allows students to provide feedback about the online course-rating system. One way in which student feedback is acknowledged is through the use of broadcasted e-mail messages in which the dean responds to concerns expressed by students (McGourty, Scoles, and Thorpe, 2002b). As faculty and students have ownership in the system itself, they appear to be more willing to use it (see Chapter Eight in this volume for the description of a highly developed feedback-reflection system).

Create a Convenient System. As mentioned earlier, convenience is not an inherent part of online course-rating systems. The features of an online rating system have to be carefully thought through and designed to make it easy for participants to use the system. Researchers have suggested the following elements of an effective, user-friendly, online course-rating system: ease of access and navigation; an attractive, simple, and straightforward screen; help features to assist with possible problems; confirmation of successful submission of the rating form; and the availability of a printable rating form in a usable format in case the form cannot be submitted electronically (Cummings, Ballantyne, and Fowler, 2001).

Create a Secure System. For students and teachers to have confidence in an online course-ratings system, they need to know that the system is secure. Students need to know that their responses are anonymous or at least confidential (that is, the author of a given comment cannot be identified or respondent identity is not accessible to those viewing rating reports). Existing literature does not seem to distinguish pointedly between anonymity and confidentiality with regard to student feedback. However, the difference between the two concepts is important enough that institutions considering online course ratings need to clarify how they will ensure anonymity or confidentiality of student feedback.

Increase Response Rates. Pioneers of online course ratings have used various approaches to ensure adequate response rates. Their experiences indicate that promotional efforts, incentives, reminders, communication to faculty and students regarding the online system, and communication to students about the use of their feedback tend to be effective methods for increasing response rates (see Chapter Five in this volume for an in-depth analysis of this issue).

Distinguish Between Means and Purpose. Paper-pencil course ratings and online course ratings are two processes (or means) aimed at fulfilling the same purpose—to obtain valid, reliable student feedback on courses and their instructors. When comparing these two modes of data collection, there is the lurking danger of losing sight of the purpose for which these systems are used. This may result in paying undue attention to some issues at the expense of overlooking other more important issues. For example, online ratings have a quicker turnaround time than the paper-pencil rating. However, as Theall (2000) notes, "putting student ratings systems online purely for supposed efficiency will do nothing to improve the poor state of evaluation practice. It will only allow bad information to be misinterpreted and misused more rapidly by those who presently do so in paper-based systems" (p. 3).

Consequently, it is important to understand that although online ratings may alleviate some of the problems of the paper-based systems, other problems exist that cannot be solved through the initiation of a new medium for data collection and reporting. Failure to recognize the limitations of the online course-rating system may obscure its users' view of those problems related to course rating that are *not* solvable through the use of an online course rating but that have to be addressed in other ways.

Collaboration and Conclusion

Those currently using or intending to use online course ratings can benefit from the experience and research of other institutions. This volume provides help in charting previously uncharted seas. Its authors, "early adopters" of online course ratings, provide valuable insights and tools to others who contemplate sailing the same seas. The Web site for Online Student Evaluation of Teaching (OnSET), hosted by the BYU Faculty Center, is another worthwhile navigation tool (see http://OnSET.byu.edu).

As campuses learn from and with one another, they increase the likelihood of successfully initiating and meeting the challenges of effective online student ratings of instruction. Then, as experience with this new collection method grows, planners and implementers will have ample opportunity for local studies and publication of this research. To guard against each campus "reinventing the (proverbial) wheel," collaboration is a byword for success.

References

Ballantyne, C. "Why Survey Online? A Practical Look at Issues in the Use of the Internet for Surveys in Higher Education." Paper presented at the annual conference of the American Evaluation Association, Honolulu, Nov. 2000. [http://www.tlc.murdoch. edu.au/pubs/docs/aea-2000.html]. Access date: Mar. 28, 2003.

Beckhard, R., and Harris, R. T. *Organizational Transitions: Managing Complex Change.* Reading, Mass.: Addison-Wesley, 1977.

Braskamp, L. A., and Ory, J. C. *Assessing Faculty Work.* San Francisco: Jossey-Bass, 1994.

Burke, W. W. *Organizational Change: Theory and Practice.* Thousand Oaks, Calif.: Sage Publications, 2002.

Cashin, W. E. "Student Ratings of Teaching: The Research Revisited." IDEA Paper No. 32. Manhattan, KS: Center for Faculty Evaluation and Development, Kansas State University, 1995. [http://www.idea.ksu.edu/papers/Idea_Paper_32.pdf]. Access date: Sep. 2, 2003.

Clark, S. J. "Results of a Web Search: Institutions of Higher Education Reporting the Use of Online Student Ratings (Summer 2003)." Provo, Utah: Brigham Young University Faculty Center, 2003 (Unpublished report).

Cummings, R., Ballantyne, C., and Fowler, L. "Online Student Feedback Surveys: Encouraging Staff and Student Use." In E. Santhanam (ed.), *Student Feedback on Teaching: Reflections and Projections, Refereed Proceedings of Teaching Evaluation Forum, August 2000, University of Western Australia* (pp. 29–37). Crawley: University of Western Australia, 2001. [http://www.csd.uwa.edu.au/spot/forum/forum_mono-graph.pdf]. Access date: Mar. 28, 2003.

Dommeyer, C. J., Baum, P., and Hanna, R. W. "College Students' Attitudes Toward Methods of Collecting Teaching Evaluation: In-Class Versus On-Line (Electronic Version)." *Journal of Education for Business,* 2002, 78(1), 5–11.

Fink, L. D. *Creating Significant Learning Experiences.* San Francisco: Jossey-Bass, 2003.

Goodman, A., and Campbell, M. "Developing Appropriate Administrative Support for Online Teaching with an Online Unit Evaluation System," 1999. [http://www. deakin.edu.au/~agoodman/isimade99.html]. Access date: Mar. 28, 2003.

Ha, T. S., and Marsh, J. "Using the Web for Student Evaluation of Teaching (COSSET and OSTEI)." n.d. [http://home.ust.hk/~eteval/cosset/qtlconf.pdf]. Access date: Mar. 28, 2003.

Hardy, N. "Perceptions of Online Evaluations: Fact and Fiction." Presented at the annual meeting of the American Educational Research Association, New Orleans, Apr. 2002.

Hmieleski, K. "Barriers to Online Evaluation: Surveying the Nation's Top 200 Most Wired Colleges." Troy, N.Y.: Interactive and Distance Education Assessment (IDEA) Laboratory, Rensselaer Polytechnic Institute, 2000 (Unpublished Report).

Hmieleski, K., and Champagne, M. V. "Plugging into Course Evaluation," 2000. [http:// ts.mivu. org/default.asp?show=article&id=795]. Access date: Mar. 28, 2003.

Johnson, T. D. "Online Student Ratings: Research and Possibilities." Invited plenary at the Online Assessment Conference, Champaign, Ill., Sept. 2001.

Johnson, T. D. "Online Student Ratings: Will Students Respond?" Presented at the annual meeting of the American Educational Research Association, New Orleans, Apr. 2002.

Knapper, C., and Cranton, P. (eds.). *Fresh Approaches to the Evaluation of Teaching.* New Directions for Teaching and Learning, no. 88. San Francisco: Jossey-Bass, 2001.

Layne, B. H., DeCristoforo, J. R., and McGinty, D. "Electronic Versus Traditional Student Ratings of Instruction (Electronic Version)." *Research in Higher Education,* 1999, 40(2), 221–232.

Lewis, K. G. (ed.). *Techniques and Strategies for Interpreting Student Evaluations.* New Directions for Teaching and Learning, no. 87. San Francisco: Jossey-Bass, 2001.

Llewellyn, D. C. "Online Reporting of Student Course Survey Results—Methods, Benefits and Concerns." Presented at the annual meeting of the American Educational Research Association, New Orleans, Apr. 2002.

Machiavelli, N. *The Prince* (H. C. Mansfield, trans.). University of Chicago Press, 1985. (Originally published 1513).

McGourty, J., Scoles, K., and Thorpe, S. "Web-Based Student Evaluation of Instruction: Promises and Pitfalls." Paper presented at the 42nd Annual Forum of the Association for Institutional Research, Toronto, Ontario, June 2002a. [http://www.drexel. edu/provost/ir/conf/webeval.pdf]. Access date: Mar. 21, 2003.

McGourty, J., Scoles, K., and Thorpe, S. "Web-Based Student Evaluation: Comparing the Experience at Two Universities." Paper presented at the 32nd Annual Frontiers in Education Conference of the American Society for Engineering Education and the Institute of Electrical and Electronics Engineers, Boston, Nov. 2002b. [http://fie. engrng.pitt.edu/fie2002/papers/1328.pdf]. Access date: Mar. 21, 2003.

McKeachie, W. J., and Kaplan, M. "Persistent Problems in Evaluating College Teaching." *AAHE Bulletin*, Feb. 5, 1996, 48(6), 5–8.

Ory, J. C. "Teaching Evaluation: Past, Present, and Future." In K. E. Ryan (ed.), *Evaluating Teaching in Higher Education: A Vision for the Future*. New Directions for Teaching and Learning, no. 83. San Francisco: Jossey-Bass, 2000, pp. 13–18.

O'Toole, J. *Leading Change: Overcoming the Ideology of Comfort and the Tyranny of Custom*. San Francisco: Jossey-Bass, 1995.

Ravelli, B. "Anonymous Online Teaching Assessments: Preliminary Findings," 2000. [http://www.edrs.com/DocLibrary/0201/ED445069.pdf]. Access date: Mar. 28, 2003.

Ryan, K. E. (ed.). *Evaluating Teaching in Higher Education: A Vision for the Future*. New Directions for Teaching and Learning, no. 83. San Francisco: Jossey-Bass, 2000.

Theall, M. "Electronic Course Evaluation Is Not Necessarily the Solution," 2000. [http://ts.mivu.org/default.asp?show=article&id=823]. Access date: Sep. 9, 2003.

Theall, M. "Student Ratings: Myths vs. Research Evidence." *Focus on Faculty*. Provo, Utah: Brigham Young University, Fall 2002. [http://www.byu.edu/fc/pages/tchlrn-pages/focusnewsletters/Focus_Fall_2002.pdf]. Access date: Aug. 26, 2003.

Theall, M., Abrami, P. C., and Mets, L. A. (eds.). *The Student Ratings Debate: Are They Valid? How Can We Best Use Them?* New Directions for Institutional Research, no. 109. San Francisco: Jossey-Bass, 2001.

Theall, M., and Franklin, J. L. "Student Ratings in the Context of Complex Evaluation Systems." In M. Theall and J. Franklin (eds.), *Student Ratings of Instruction: Issues for Improving Practice*. New Directions for Teaching and Learning, no. 43, San Francisco: Jossey-Bass, 1990.

Thorpe, S. "Online Student Evaluation of Instruction: An Investigation of Non-Response Bias." Paper presented at the 42nd Annual Forum of the Association for Institutional Research, Toronto, Canada, June 2002. [http://airweb.org/forum02/550.pdf]. Access date: Mar. 28, 2003.

Tichy, N. M. *Managing Strategic Change: Technical, Political and Cultural Dynamics*. New York: John Wiley and Sons, 1983.

Tichy, N. M., and Sherman, S. *Control Your Destiny or Someone Else Will*. New York: HarperCollins, 1994.

Weimer, M. *Learner-Centered Teaching*. San Francisco: Jossey-Bass, 2002.

Zimitat, C., and Crebert, G. "Conducting Online Research and Evaluation." In A. Goody, J. Herrington, and M. Northcote (eds.), *Research and Development in Higher Education—Vol. 25: Quality Conversations. Refereed Proceedings of the Annual International HERDSA Conference 7–10 July 2002, Perth, Western Australia,* 2002. Canberra, Australia: Higher Education Research and Development Society of Australasia. [http://www.ecu.edu.au/conferences/herdsa/main/papers/ref/pdf/ Zimitat.pdf]. Access date: Mar. 28, 2003.

D. Lynn Sorenson is assistant director of the Brigham Young University Faculty Center in Provo, Utah.

Christian Reiner is assessment and evaluation specialist at the Purdue University Center for Instructional Excellence in West Lafayette, Indiana.

Appendix to Chapter 1. Web Sites of Institutions That Use Online Student Ratings of Instruction

Institution	Web Address(es)
Air Force Academy Colorado Springs, CO	Report of issues involved in administering all mid-course and end-of-course surveys online http://home.att.net/bobewell/oleval.htm
Arizona State University Tempe, AZ	College of Engineering and Applied Sciences online ratings https://intraweb.eas.asu.edu/eval
Boise State University Boise, ID	Online Course Evaluation page http://coeneval.boisestate.edu EDTech Online Rating Form http://edtech.boisestate.edu/resources/online_eval/default.htm
Brigham Young University* Provo, UT	Faculty resources for online student ratings http://www.byu.edu/fc/pages/tchlrnpages/onlinestudentratings.html
Carnegie Mellon University Pittsburg, PA	Faculty Course Evaluations (FCE system) www.cmu.edu:8001/hub/online_services.html FCE information http://www.cmu.edu:8001/hub/fce_faculty.html
Columbia University New York City, NY	Web-Based Course Evaluation System (WCES) Overview http://oracle.seas.columbia.edu/wces/about/overview.php
Ferris State University Big Rapids, Michigan	Online SAI (Student Assessment of Instruction) http://www.ferris.edu/htmls/administration/academicaffairs/vpoffice/word_docs/sairecommendations.doc
Georgia Institute of Technology* Atlanta, GA	Course-Instructor Opinion Survey (CIOS) information https://intranet.gatech.edu/cfprod/cios/student_general_help.html Frequently Asked Questions http://www.cetl.gatech.edu/menu_options/cios/CIOSFAQ.htm
Hong Kong University of Science and Technology Hong Kong, China	COSSET (Centralized On-line System for Summative Evaluation of Teaching) information page http://celt.ust.hk/teach_in_ust/evaluation.htm
Indiana University Bloomington, IN	Custom online evaluation using QuizSite www.indiana.edu/best/course_evaluations.shtml
Indiana Wesleyan University Marion, IN	Student log-in page for online evaluations http://survey.indwes.edu
Medical College of Wisconsin	Student instructions http://www.mcw.edu/gradschool/handbook/courseevals.htm
Memorial University of New Foundland, St. John's, Canada	http://www.mun.ca/
Montana State University Billings, MT	Course and Instructor Evaluation Form www.msubillings.edu/support101/eCollege/courseevaluation.htm
Mount Royal College Calgary, Alberta, Canada	Free Assessment Survey Tool (FAST) www2.mtroyal.ab.ca/bravelli
Murdoch University Perth, Western Australia	Student Surveys of Teaching and Units http://www.tlc.murdoch.edu.au/eddev/evaluation/survey/frontpage.html

Appendix to Chapter 1. Continued

Institution	Web Address(es)
Northwestern University* Evanston, IL	Online course evaluations (Department of Physics and Astronomy) http://dirac.phys.northwestern.edu/anderson/courses/ctec.html
Pennsylvania State University State College, PA	Instruction Evaluation Sheet http://espse.ed.psu.edu/espse/hale/507mat/CourseInfo/SRTE.html
Polytechnic University Brooklyn, NY	Sample Course Evaluation (Ceval) form http://survey.poly.edu/Ceval/CevalSp.shtml
Purdue University West Lafayette, IN	Purdue Online Evaluation (POLE) home page http://sotdev6.tech.purdue.edu/cgt-eval/
Rice University Houston, TX	Post-Semester Student Survey http://dacnet.rice.edu/courseeval/survey/students.cfm
Smith College Northampton, MA	Recommendations for student evaluation of courses at Smith College http://www.smith.edu/deanoffaculty/Al.html
University of Cincinnati Cincinnati, OH	Department of Germanic Languages and Literatures sample online form http://asweb.artsci.uc.edu/forms_scripts/germanlang/german_form_grad.cfm
University of Colorado Boulder, CO	Faculty Course Questionnaire (FCQ) information page http://www.colorado.edu/pba/fcq/
University of Delaware Newark, DE	Project notes and mock-up for doing Web-based course evaluations http://www.udel.edu/lynam/course-evals/
University of Hawaii Honolulu, HI	Electronic evaluation of astronomy graduate courses home.hawaii.rr.com/intermatter/evaluations.htm
University of Idaho Moscow, ID	Informational site for the University of Idaho's Online Student Evaluations of Teaching http://www.webs.uidaho.edu/studentevals/
University of Illinois* Urbana-Champaign. IL Chicago, IL	Evaluation Online (EON) http://www.oir.uiuc.edu/dme/eon/ http://www.oir.uiuc.edu/dme/eon/request/index.cfm Online course evaluation form for UIC Radon Course on Migation http://www.uic.edu/sph/glakes/radon_course/final/evaluation.asp
University of Kansas Medical Center Kansas City, KS	School of Nursing student instructions http://www2.kumc.edu/nursing/nursingeval/evcourses/evaluation.htm
University of North Carolina Chapel Hill, NC	Dental Department http://www.dent.unc.edu/academic
University of Northern Iowa Cedar Falls, IA	University of Northern Iowa Student Evaluation of Teaching (UNISET) http://access.uni.edu/acad/uniset.html
University of North Texas Science Center, Fort Worth, Texas	University of North Texas Science Center http://www.hsc.unt.edu/education/edsupport.cfm
University of Prince Edward Island, Charlottetown, PE	Department of Music Student Ratings of Instruction http://www.upei.ca/musicd/academic/sri.html

Appendix to Chapter 1. Continued

Institution	Web Address(es)
Western Washington University Bellingham, WA	Instructions for using teaching evaluation forms http://www.ac.wwu.edu/assess/tval.htm
Wellesley College Wellesley, MA	Student Evaluation Questionnaire (SEQ) http://www.wellesley.edu/
Whitman College Walla Walla, WA	Online Course Evaluation help and instructions https://www.whitman.edu/evals/
Yale University New Haven, CN	Yale Herald article about the Online Course Critique http://www.yaleherald.com/article.php?Article521

*Authors at these universities have written chapters in this volume of *New Directions for Teaching and Learning*.

Source: From Clark, S. J. "Use of Online Student Ratings at Institutions of Higher Education: Results of a Web Search." Provo, Utah: Faculty Center, Brigham Young University, 2003. Institutions listed here use online systems to evaluate face-to-face courses for departments, colleges, divisions, or entire campuses (does not include campus systems in which only online courses are rated online). An expanded list of institutions using online student ratings can be found at the Web site for Online Student Evaluation of Teaching, hosted by the Brigham Young University Faculty Center: http://OnSET.byu.edu. The Web site includes resources for those considering or researching online student ratings.

*Many U.S. institutions of higher education are initiating
and expanding the use of the Internet for collecting and
reporting student ratings of instruction.*

Online Course Evaluation and Reporting in Higher Education

Kevin M. Hoffman

The Internet has revolutionized the world of higher education. Long-standing and laborious institutional processes have been streamlined or replaced. From student information systems to online registration, the Internet has transformed (and is continuing to transform) the ways in which information is collected, processed, and distributed within institutions.

Online student evaluations of instruction have received increasing attention over the past few years. In 2000, Hmieleski surveyed the nation's two hundred most wired institutions regarding the use of the Internet in evaluating teaching. At that time, he found that 98 percent of responding institutions still used paper-based methods as their predominant approach to student evaluation. The use of the Internet for evaluating teaching was extremely limited outside of distance-education programs. However, since Hmieleski's study, the number of studies and articles about online student evaluations has been growing (Cantera, 2002; Mayer and George, 2003; McGourty, Scoles, and Thorpe, 2002). Given the prevalence of the Internet in higher education (Green, 2002) and the growing literature about online student evaluation, the following question naturally arises: How prevalent is today's use of the Internet for student evaluation of course and instruction in higher education?

The primary objective of the present study is to better understand the effects of the Internet on student ratings of instruction in higher education. More specifically, data were collected to determine the extent to which institutions have adopted the Internet for data collection and reporting of student evaluations of instruction.

Method

For this study, a sample of five hundred U.S. colleges and universities was randomly selected from the U.S. institutions listed in the 2002 Higher Education Directory (Burke, 2002). Researchers identified directors of assessment, evaluation, and institutional research (or those in similar positions) at each of the five hundred institutions. Contact information for these individuals was sought through the institutions' Web sites and using published lists of various professional organizations. In some cases, when an appropriate title could not be identified, a vice president of academic affairs or provost was contacted.

The questionnaire developed for this study included a scale that examined the institution's adoption of the Internet for various aspects of the student ratings process. In each of the survey areas, participants were asked to select from the following five possible responses: "doing this already," "will implement in 2003," "reviewing in 2003," "decided not to do this," or "not applicable" (N.A.).

E-mail invitations were sent to the five hundred institutions requesting participation in the study. A Web link was imbedded in the e-mail message that allowed respondents to click on the link and go directly to the online questionnaire. The questionnaire was available between October 2002 and the end of December 2002. All respondents were entered into a raffle to win a $100 Amazon.com gift certificate. During the survey period, two reminder notifications were sent to the nonrespondents encouraging their participation in the survey. At the end of the two-month survey period, a total of 256 respondents had completed the questionnaire.

Survey Results

Results of the survey are categorized into the following four areas: primary method used to conduct student evaluations, Internet collection of student evaluation data, Internet reporting of student evaluation results to faculty, and Internet reporting of student evaluation results to students.

Primary Method Used to Conduct Student Evaluations. Respondents were asked to report the primary method used to collect student evaluation feedback at their institutions. Ten percent indicated that a campuswide Internet system was the principal means of collecting student-ratings data for all courses. This finding suggests that since Hmieleski's study in 2000, there has been approximately an 8 percent increase in the use of Internet systems as institutions' primary means for student evaluation of instruction. Ninety percent of responding institutions reported using some type of a paper-based process; 78 percent used scannable paper forms, and another 12 percent used nonscannable paper forms.

Internet Collection of Student Evaluation Data. Survey participants were asked to report on the use of the Internet for collecting student evaluation data in online courses and face-to-face courses. This approach was designed to separate results regarding face-to-face courses from results regarding online courses. This allowed researchers to differentiate between online evaluation of online courses and online evaluation of face-to-face courses.

Online Evaluation of Online Courses. In 2002, nearly two-thirds of the survey respondents indicated either that they were already using the Internet for evaluating online courses (56 percent) or that they would implement an Internet ratings process in 2003 (10 percent). The remaining respondents were reviewing this as an option for online courses (18 percent), or they had decided not to use the Internet to evaluate online courses (16 percent).

Online Evaluation of Face-to-Face Courses. Of the responding institutions, 17 percent reported using the Internet in some capacity to collect student evaluation data for face-to-face courses. This percentage was higher than previous findings in this area (Hmieleski, 2000) and suggests that using the Internet for student evaluation of face-to-face courses has increased. In addition, another 10 percent indicated that their institutions planned to initiate Internet evaluations of face-to-face courses in 2003. Eighteen percent of the respondents were in the process of reviewing Internet options. The remainder had decided against using the Internet for collecting student feedback.

Statistical Comparison. Researchers in the study hypothesized that Internet use for student evaluation of online courses would be higher than in face-to-face courses. To test this hypothesis, a χ^2 analysis was used to determine if the proportion of respondents who indicated that they used the Internet to evaluate online courses was significantly different from the proportion of institutions using the Internet to evaluate face-to-face courses. The results of the analysis revealed that there was in fact a difference in the two proportions with a significant $\chi^2(1, N = 512) = 95.68$, $p < .001$. According to these data, more institutions were found to be using the Internet for student ratings of online courses than for face-to-face courses.

Internet Reporting of Student Evaluations to Faculty. Hmieleski (2000) suggested that when student evaluations were put online, the corresponding reporting of results to faculty was also put online. The present study tested this assumption. Twenty-two percent of the respondents reported using the Internet to provide faculty with access to student rating results for face-to-face courses; another 11 percent planned to do so in 2003. The remaining respondents either were reviewing online reporting as an option (30 percent) or had decided not to do so (38 percent).

A χ^2 analysis was used to determine if the proportion of respondents using the Internet to provide faculty with data from student ratings was different from the proportion of respondents using the Internet to collect data from students. The χ^2 analysis revealed a significant difference between the use of the Internet for collecting student evaluation data and for reporting these results to faculty online: $\chi^2(1, N = 511) = 6.21, p < .05$. Thus, it appears that institutions are using the Internet more widely to provide results of course evaluations to faculty than for collecting data from students.

Internet Reporting of Student Evaluations to Students. In addition to faculty access to student evaluation feedback, students have access to evaluation results in paper form at some institutions. Given the ease of communicating information by the Internet, it is plausible that some institutions would elect to share student evaluation results with the students through the Internet. To examine this possibility, survey respondents were asked to report if and how they used the Internet to share evaluation results with students. Twelve percent of the overall respondent group reported already using the Internet to share student evaluation results with students. Another 3 percent planned to implement online reporting of results to students in 2003. Eighteen percent of respondents reported that they were considering this option; however, most respondents (67 percent) had no plans to share student evaluation results with students through the Internet. (For more information on Internet reporting of student evaluations to students, see Chapters Three and Eight in this volume.)

Conclusion

As the use of the Internet continues to expand within higher education, institutions are implementing Web-based systems for both collecting and reporting student evaluation data. Paper-based evaluation remains the predominant method of data collection in face-to-face courses; nevertheless, this study found an increase of approximately 8 percent since 2000 in the use of the Internet as a primary means of collecting student feedback. Furthermore, researchers found that many institutions were either planning to implement or considering implementation of online student evaluations in 2003.

This study also found that a number of institutions use both paper-based and online methods for collecting student evaluation feedback. At these institutions, online courses are increasingly being evaluated online, and the number of face-to-face courses evaluated online has increased.

Perhaps one of the more interesting findings of this study is the degree to which the Internet is being used to report results of student evaluations. Before the study, researchers assumed that institutions were using the Internet equally to collect and report course evaluation data. Researchers were surprised to discover, however, that Internet distribution of student evaluation reports to faculty was more common than the use of the Internet for collecting student-rating data. The data from this study suggest that both online data collection and online reporting are growing in popularity.

Another unexpected finding from this study was the extent to which institutions may use the Internet to share student evaluation results with students. There has been little information about the prevalence of sharing rating results with students, either on paper or online, but this study begins to quantify how common this practice has become through the Internet. Future research in this area will offer further insights into trends of sharing results with students, both what has been done in the past in printed form and what can be done in the future using the Internet.

The question is not whether the Internet will be used for collection and reporting of student evaluation data; rather, the question is, to what extent will institution-wide processes be transformed to the online environment, and how rapidly will this occur?

References

Burke, J. *2002 Higher Education Directory*. Falls Church, Va.: Higher Education Publications, 2002.

Cantera, L. "Y Puts Teacher Evaluations Online." *NewsNet* by Brigham Young University, 2002. [http://newsnet.byu.edu/story.cfm/41005]. Access date: Aug. 26, 2003.

Green, K. "The 2002 National Survey of Information Technology in U.S. Higher Education." Report prepared by the Campus Computing Project, Encino, Calif., Oct. 2002. [http://www.campuscomputing.net/summaries/2002/index.html]. Access date: Aug. 26, 2003.

Hmieleski, K. "Barriers to Online Evaluation: Surveying the Nation's Top 200 Most Wired Colleges." Troy, N.Y.: Interactive and Distance Education Assessment Laboratory, Rensselaer Polytechnic Institute, 2000 (Unpublished Report).

Mayer, J., and George, A. "The University of Idaho's Online Course Evaluation System: Going Forward!" Paper presented at the 43rd Annual Forum of the Association for Institutional Research, Tampa, Fla., May 2003.

McGourty, J., Scoles, K., and Thorpe, S. "Web-Based Student Evaluation of Instruction: Promises and Pitfalls." Paper presented at the 42nd Annual Forum of the Association for Institutional Research, Toronto, Ontario, June 2002.

KEVIN M. HOFFMAN is director of evaluation services at eCollege.com, a company that provides electronic learning solutions to online degree programs.

Northwestern University's experience sheds light on some of the common (mis)perceptions about online student evaluations.

Online Ratings: Fact and Fiction

When Northwestern University (Evanston, Illinois) put forth the idea of using the Web to collect student ratings of instruction, the proposal was met with fear and skepticism by most segments of the university community. Some felt that the time-honored course evaluations would be desecrated by using the Web. Students seemed certain they would lose the anonymity they had always presumed when completing their evaluations on paper. Instructors and administrators worried that students would not complete their evaluations unless they were held captive in class to do so. Across campus, there was a generalized faculty fear that the only students who would respond online were those with strong negative opinions of a class or instructor.

Background

At Northwestern University, evaluations have been collected by the Course and Teacher Evaluation Council (CTEC) for more than twenty years. Although these evaluations can be customized (for example, by instructor, department, or college), the following items are common to all questionnaires: five core (general) questions, four open-ended questions (for example, strengths, weaknesses, or suggestions), and the "summary comments" in which students summarize their responses to the four open-ended questions. These paper rating forms were used by Northwestern University before 1999, when experimentation with online collection began. By that time, data entry had progressed from manual entry to the use of scan forms. Processing the paper evaluations—including scanning numerical responses, typing the summary comments, and reporting results—was a cumbersome process that took from ten to twelve weeks. The new online system has improved this process; evaluation information is now available to instructors as soon as they have submitted their grades for the quarter to the registrar's office. Through the years, numerical scores and student comments have been made available to the university community—in the past, with an annual publication the students could purchase and most recently by online postings.

For years, students have used evaluation data during registration to assist them in selecting their courses and instructors. Now, using the online system, students sit at their computers to register for their classes with one window open to the registration site and another open to the evaluation site. In addition, instructors rely heavily on their student evaluations to improve their teaching and restructure their courses; administrators rely on the evaluations to assist in curricular changes and in making promotion and tenure decisions.

Although the initial idea of online student evaluations sent waves of fear across campus, there were also strong advocates who wanted to see online student ratings eventually replace the cumbersome paper-collection method. One of the most appealing aspects of the online system was the immediate availability of results. Many instructors also welcomed recovering class time formerly used in administering evaluations.

Amid both support and resistance, Northwestern University began collecting most evaluations online for the spring quarter of the 1999–2000 academic year. At that time, new policy dictated that all courses be evaluated online unless instructors specifically requested the traditional paper evaluation forms for their classes. The new online evaluation form mirrors the paper evaluation form; it has the same questions and format, which allows integration of the evaluation reports from both systems. Since implementation of the new system, students have become convinced that online evaluations may actually be more anonymous than submitting their handwritten comments on the paper forms. Students seem to prefer submitting evaluations online rather than writing them on paper.

Student Rating Scores

During the early implementation phase of the Web-based system, perceptions (and misperceptions) surfaced about online ratings of instruction, some of which are discussed below.

> PERCEPTION: Results will be (or are) lower for online ratings than for paper ratings.
> REALITY: The ratings may be (somewhat) lower.

One professor on campus contacted CTEC with a request for data to do a study in which he might show that online ratings are lower than paper-pencil ratings. The CTEC office complied and supplied him with data collected from online and from paper forms for fall quarter 1999 through fall quarter 2000 (the first four quarters in which online ratings were used). The study was conducted during the summer of 2001 and included data from 5,112 classes (2,457 classes had used paper forms, and 2,655 classes had used online forms).

The comparison of the data indicated that the overall online scores were 0.25 of a point lower than the paper scores on the six-point scale of 1 (low) to 6 (high). This professor then requested that identifiers be included in the study because he believed the difference in scores would become substantially larger if further analyses were done comparing online versions with paper versions from the exact same classes (same instructor, same course), including evaluations done both ways. The effect of the second study was exactly the same: 0.25 of a point lower (on a six-point scale) for online evaluations.

REALITY: The ratings may be lower or higher or the same.

To further examine the relationship of online and paper ratings, the CTEC conducted its own comparison studies—one at the end of fall quarter 2001 and another after spring quarter 2002. For this study, CTEC examined twenty-six classes in which the same instructor taught the same class multiple times, using both paper and online evaluations. The comparison involved the five core questions on the evaluation form, which are general questions asked about every class at Northwestern. The group of classes used for the study is representative of all the undergraduate schools within the university, with class sizes ranging from four to 634 students.

The twenty-six classes in the comparison study were taught a total of 274 times between fall quarter 1996 and spring quarter 2002. Paper forms were used to evaluate 135 classes, and online evaluations were conducted on 139 classes. Each class was evaluated with only paper or only online evaluations; collection methods were never mixed within the same class. Every course was evaluated at least twice—and some up to thirty-seven times—using one or the other collection method.

Among the courses included in the study, eleven average scores from online evaluations were higher than the average scores from paper evaluations (on the five core items). Twelve courses' average scores from paper evaluations were higher than the average scores from the online ratings (on the five core items). For three of the courses, the average scores were mixed, with some of the items rated higher on paper and some rated higher online (see Figure 3.1).

Student Comments

PERCEPTION: "[I prefer using paper forms because] people are more likely to write comments [on paper], and the response rate is everyone in class. . . ." [Comment by a teacher of a large introductory course, as quoted in the student newspaper]

Figure 3.1. Comparison of Results for Online and Paper Ratings, Same Class Taught by Same Instructor

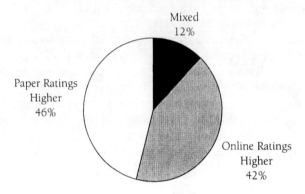

REALITY: One large introductory course registered little difference between the number and length of student comments, whether online or on paper.

In a review of seven sections of this large introductory course (ranging in size from 432 to 634 students), five of the classes were evaluated using paper, and two were evaluated online. Both the number of students commenting and the length of student comments were comparable for paper and online evaluations. In fact, the above-mentioned instructor usually elicits extensive favorable comments, regardless of the method of data collection. (The overall response rate for paper evaluations in this teacher's course was 54 percent, and the overall response rate for online evaluations was 48.5 percent.)

REALITY: Substantially more written comments are submitted online.

In another study, six classes with similar content were examined within the same department. The enrollment of each class was between thirty-nine and forty-three students. Four of the classes were evaluated online, and two were evaluated using paper forms. First, the overall response rates of all classes were compared. (The overall response rate included all students who responded to any portion of an evaluation for the class.) Then, the number of student comments was compared. The summary comments seem to be the most important to students because they are posted on the Web for university-wide review. A compilation of these summary comments is also included with the numerical report that is returned to the instructor, the department chair, and the dean.

One class using paper forms had an enrollment of forty-three students. This class had a response rate of 100 percent; all forty-three students responded to at least some part of the rating form. However, only seven of the

Figure 3.2. Response Rates for Classes Evaluated on Paper and Those Evaluated Online

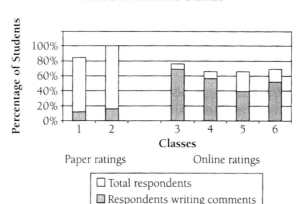

forty-three responding students (16 percent) wrote comments. These seven students wrote a total of nine lines of text about the class. The second class using paper evaluation had responses from thirty-three of the forty students enrolled, for an overall response rate of 83 percent. Only four of those thirty-three students (12 percent) wrote summary comments, generating a total of six lines of text.

Then the classes using paper rating forms were compared with the classes evaluated online. The overall response rate in the classes evaluated online was somewhat lower. However, students wrote many more comments when they rated courses online. One of the online classes with an enrollment of forty students had responses from twenty-nine students (73 percent). Nineteen of these twenty-nine student respondents (66 percent) completed the summary comments, generating sixty-three lines of text. The other three classes evaluated online had similar results. The overall response rates of the online classes ranged from 64 through 69 percent. The number of students who completed the summary question ranged from 37 percent to 48 percent, resulting in proportionate increases in the amount of text written. On average, classes evaluated online had more than five times as much written commentary as the classes evaluated on paper, despite the slightly lower overall response rates for the classes evaluated online (Figure 3.2). The more extensive comments collected online provide a valuable resource for instructors who want to improve teaching and learning in their classes.

PERCEPTION: In comparison with comments written on paper rating forms, students write more negative comments when they submit responses online.

REALITY: Students submit positive, negative, and mixed comments online.

Students tend to be more expansive in their comments when they enter them online at their convenience. However, there is a division of thought regarding the nature of these comments. Some faculty members believed that online rating systems encourage students to be less hurried and more contemplative when entering their comments; others felt that students' isolation and the anonymity of the online environment would promote negative student comments.

The subjective nature of student comments makes them more difficult to measure than numerical ratings. To quantify comments, CTEC researchers classified each comment as positive, negative, or mixed. The comments were classified using each student's response in its entirety to the summary question. Student comments were classified as positive or negative when everything written tended in that direction. Responses classified as mixed contained both positive and negative elements. For example, a student may have commented favorably about most elements of the class but indicated one area that needed improvement. Compared with courses that were evaluated using paper forms, comments written about courses that were evaluated online showed no tendency toward more negative or mean-spirited responses.

In comparing the six courses evaluated online and on paper, the number of positive, negative, and mixed comments was similar. In fact, two of the online classes had a higher percentage of positive comments than the classes evaluated on paper, which contradicted the preconception about online ratings. One of these classes using online evaluations was taught by a first-year instructor. The students seemed to be sensitive to the teacher's first-year status and tended to give more mixed comments of a forgiving nature and to offer suggestions for improvements in the future. Although one of the classes evaluated online had a higher percentage of negative than positive comments, this would be expected within any sampling of classes (see Figure 3.3 for a distribution of the subjective quality of summary essay comments).

Conclusion

After decades of paper-pencil evaluations, Northwestern University implemented a system for online student ratings of instruction in 1999. Since then, students have evaluated instruction online and have obtained a certain portion of the compiled reports through the Web. More portions of the evaluation report are made available online to faculty and administrators.

Although some skeptics were resistant to the change to online course ratings, many (mis)perceptions have been dispelled by the realities of the Northwestern online ratings experience; for example, average numerical scores for the online ratings have been shown to be about the same as for the paper ratings. Although response rates have been somewhat lower using the online system, those students who do respond write more detailed

Figure 3.3. Distribution of Positive, Negative, and Mixed Comments

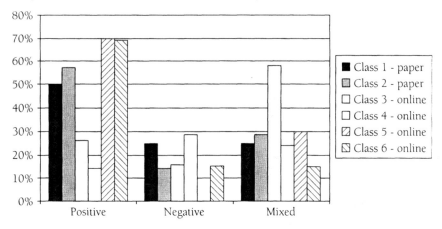

comments online. These additional comments are a valuable resource to instructors who want to improve teaching and learning in their classes. Overall, the reality of the online ratings experience at Northwestern has motivated administrators, faculty, staff, and students to continue online data collection and online reporting for student ratings of instruction.

Questions for Further Investigation

Online student ratings of instruction are in their infancy and invite a great deal of study and improvement. As CTEC continues to collect evaluations, predominantly through the electronic process, important questions will need to be answered.

So far at Northwestern, response rates for the online evaluations have been somewhat lower than those for paper evaluations. Is it possible to collect evaluations electronically with close to the same response rate as those collected using paper rating forms? Under what conditions might this be achieved? Might this goal be achieved if every student sat in class with a laptop computer? How high must response rates be to establish validity?

Online ratings yield more student comments, and these comments appear to be more useful to faculty and students. Does this increase in student comments compensate for a somewhat lower response rate from the online ratings? In other words, which is more valid and useful, evaluations from a greater number of students (some of whom will write almost anything just to have it finished and leave the classroom) or collecting evaluations from fewer students who have definite ideas concerning the class and who provide more written feedback?

Do online evaluations generally yield lower scores than paper evaluations? Research conducted so far at Northwestern is inconclusive on this point. If further research shows that online ratings are lower, what are the implications? What would need to happen for the university community to accept an adjusted standard of ratings results?

These and other questions need to be answered as Northwestern and other universities explore and move forward with online student ratings of instruction.

NEDRA HARDY is senior assistant registrar at Northwestern University in Evanston, Illinois.

This study compares mean ratings, inter-rater reliabilities, and the factor structure of items for online and paper student-rating forms from the University of Washington's Instructional Assessment System.

Psychometric Properties of Student Ratings of Instruction in Online and on-Campus Courses

Debbie E. McGhee, Nana Lowell

Higher education has experienced a dramatic increase in the number of online courses and programs and an increase in the frequency with which online components are incorporated into on-campus courses (Lewis, Snow, Farris, and Levin, 1999; Green, 2001). These trends have led to the development of online systems for the collection of student ratings of instruction. Such systems offer the advantage of being easily integrated into normal online-course operations, just as traditional paper-based ratings have been integrated into traditional courses by being administered during a class period. Although there is extensive literature on the properties of student ratings collected in traditional classroom settings (for example, Cohen, 1981; Feldman, 1989; d'Apollonia and Abrami, 1997; Greenwald and Gillmore, 1997; Marsh and Roche, 1997), comparable information regarding student ratings of online courses is not widely available.

To date, few systematic studies have been done of student reactions to online courses versus traditional classroom courses. Knight, Ridley, and Davies (1998) reported that students in online sections reported putting more effort and more time into online course work than their classroom peers; yet, student satisfaction was comparable across modes. Spooner, Jordan, Algozzine, and Spooner (1999) reported that students in online and classroom courses gave similar ratings of course and instructional quality. In two studies wherein the same instructor taught both in-class and online sections of the same course, Waschull (2001) found that students who either voluntarily enrolled or were randomly assigned to an online section gave course ratings similar to those who enrolled in a traditional classroom section.

Turning to the broader question of the general comparability of questionnaire or survey data collected online versus data collected through traditional, paper-based means, there have been several promising findings. For example, Buchanan and Smith (1999) and Pasveer and Ellard (1998) obtained similar results for personality questionnaire data collected by the two modes. Stanton (1998) reported fewer missing values in personnel survey data collected by means of the World Wide Web than in paper-pencil surveys (through the mail), and the factor structures of the two sets of data were not significantly different from one another.

In this chapter, we report psychometric properties of student ratings of distance-learning courses collected online and compare them with psychometric properties of an established, paper-based system used in on-campus courses.

Instructional Assessment System

The Instructional Assessment System (IAS) is a program used to collect and summarize student ratings of instruction at the postsecondary level. Before 1972, course ratings at the University of Washington (UW) in Seattle were collected and summarized manually. To facilitate wider use of the rating program, rating forms were standardized and converted to machine-readable (scannable) format, and a computerized database was created for reporting and archiving results. At this time, the system was formally named. In the ensuing years, the system has been expanded to include a range of forms to assess a variety of instructional formats. Students complete these forms in the classroom at the end of the academic term, and the forms are then returned to a central office for processing.

Rating forms for all instructional formats include four general items relating to the course and the instructor. Most forms also include five "relative-effort" items that ask students to compare the current course with other college courses. Eighteen items address specific aspects of the course. Instructors can add class-specific items to the back of the scannable forms, and ratings are supplemented by open-ended student comments collected on a separate questionnaire. Through a set of regular reports, ratings summaries are made available to faculty for the purpose of instructional improvement and to administrators for use in retention, promotion, and tenure decisions. In addition, descriptive statistics for the four general items are reported over the Internet for easy reference by students when selecting courses. IAS item ratings show high inter-rater (class-level) reliability and interclass (instructor-level) reliability (Lowell and Gillmore, 1991; Gillmore, 2000). In sum, the IAS provides a robust system for collecting and summarizing student ratings of instruction. In addition to UW, some fifty-two institutions nationwide currently use the IAS.

IAS Online

The IAS includes a scannable form designed specifically for evaluating distance-education courses. The assessment items on this form address some of the concerns particular to the distance-learning format. The rating form is delivered through the mail in the same way the course materials are delivered. However, this method of collecting course ratings does not work well for distance-education courses taught online. Hence, in 1999, IAS Online (http://depts.washington.edu/oeaias) was created as an extension of the existing paper-based system. As does the standard IAS, the online system provides common items for cross-course comparison and allows the creation of class-specific items. It produces course reports for instructors and combined reports for program staff and builds a longitudinal database for use in historical studies. The similarities of the online and paper-based systems facilitate comparisons of courses taught and rated in different modalities.

To investigate whether IAS Online provides data of comparable substance and quality to the original IAS, the university carried out a series of analyses of items common to both formats. Note that because of the nature of the data examined in this study (see below), it is not possible to separate the effects of mode of instruction from mode of data collection. Thus, throughout the remainder of this paper, the term *online ratings* refers to student ratings of distance courses collected through the Web, and *on-campus* refers to paper-pencil ratings of classroom courses.

Method

Although IAS and IAS Online offer several different evaluation forms and items, they have eleven items in common. These are the focus of the present study. In Table 4.1, items 1 through 4 are global items that ask for student opinion on the course overall, quality of the course content, the instructor's contribution, and either the instructor's or the delivery format's effectiveness (on campus or online, respectively). Items 5 through 9 assess student effort in the course relative to other courses taken, and items 10 and 11 ask students to estimate how much time they devoted to the course on a weekly basis.

The data set for this study initially consisted of student ratings of these common questionnaire items for all courses rated during two academic years (1999–2000 and 2000–01). Student ratings were culled from the existing IAS and IAS Online databases. (On-campus courses were taught on the UW-Seattle campus, and online courses were offered through various UW distance-learning programs, foremost of which was UW Educational Outreach.) Classes in which fewer than five students provided ratings were excluded, resulting in a data set that included 18,212 on-campus classes rated by 363,044 students and sixty-five distance courses rated by 668 students. (Of course, not all students responded to every item.)

Table 4.1. Mean (SD) Item Ratings By Class Mode

		On Campus		Online			
Item no.	Item[a]	Mean	SD	Mean	SD	t[b]	df
1.	Course as a whole	4.76	1.02	4.66	1.05	2.60	379,291
2.	Course content	4.75	0.98	4.74	1.05	0.27	378,462
3.	Instructor's contribution	4.97	1.08	4.58	1.21	9.58	377,597*
4.	Instructor or delivery format effectiveness	4.82	1.15	4.40	1.14	9.21	377,129*
5.	Expected grade relative to other college courses	4.75	1.30	4.69	1.08	0.98	358,705
6.	Relative intellectual challenge of course	5.11	1.25	5.11	1.18	0	359,550
7.	Relative effort in course	5.02	1.32	5.39	1.17	−7.37	359,952*
8.	Relative effort to succeed	5.15	1.26	5.31	1.19	−3.34	358,110*
9.	Relative involvement in course	5.18	1.28	5.45	1.14	−5.54	359,036*
10.	Average hours per week spent on course	5.17	2.39	5.61	2.62	−5.95	356,618*
11.	Valuable course-work-hours per week	4.34	2.30	4.57	2.54	−2.65	357,146

[a]Items 1 through 4 were rated on a scale of 1 (very poor) to 6 (excellent), items 5 through 9 on a scale of 1 (much lower) to 7 (much higher), and items 10 and 11 on a scale of 1 (under 2 hours) to 12 (over 22 hours).

[b]To minimize the risk of capitalizing on chance, the significance level was adjusted for the number of t tests using the Bonferroni correction.

*$p < .0045$.

The analyses reported below compared the mean ratings of on-campus and online courses and determined the inter-rater reliability of ratings of individual items and of specific item clusters. On-campus and online course ratings were compared by the use of t tests on the means of each of the eleven items (Table 4.1). Because of the large number of statistical tests, α was adjusted using the Bonferroni correction, such that the critical value of p was set to .0045 (rather than the traditional .05).

Inter-rater reliability reflects the degree to which students in a particular class agree or are consistent in their ratings of a particular item. For each item, inter-rater reliability was calculated by a one-way analysis of variance, with class as the between-groups variable and student raters nested within classes as the within group. The formula $(F-1)/F$ returns the intraclass correlation coefficient (ICC) for κ equals the mean number of raters per course (Kane, Gillmore, and Crooks, 1976). Because the ICC is directly related to the number of raters, researchers estimated ICCs for various class sizes by applying the general form of the Spearman-Brown prophecy formula: $r_k = \kappa r_1 / [1 + (\kappa - 1) r_1]$, where r_1 is the reliability of one observation and r_k is the reliability of κ observations.

Finally, to examine the structural comparability of ratings obtained in the two modalities, UW researchers carried out exploratory factor analyses separately for each sample. They calculated aggregate scores and then computed inter-rater reliabilities of those aggregates.

Results

Study results are reported in three areas: comparisons of means, inter-rater reliabilities, and item clusters.

On-Campus and Online Means Comparisons. As shown in Table 4.1, average ratings tended to be skewed toward the upper ends of the scales for all items and both instructional modes. On-campus and online classes were rated similarly on five of the items (1, 2, 5, 6, and 11), whereas students in on-campus courses gave significantly higher average ratings than their online peers on two items (3 and 4) that dealt with the instructor's contribution and instructor- or delivery-format effectiveness. On the remaining four items, mean ratings were significantly higher in the online classes, indicating that students tended to rate online courses as more demanding than those taught on campus.

Inter-rater Reliabilities. With one exception, the observed inter-rater reliabilities ranged from moderate to very high (Table 4.2). Coefficients calculated directly from the on-campus data ranged from .68 (item 9) to .91 (item 10). In the online sample, the range was .31 (item 5) to .86 (item 1).

Ratings of items 1 through 3 evinced the strongest reliability across instructional modalities. For all three items in both samples, it was estimated that an acceptable level of .70 could be reached with as few as seven raters.

The *observed* reliabilities of ratings for online courses tended to be lower than those for on-campus courses, but this difference was largely due to the smaller number of raters in online courses (Ms = 19.9 on campus compared with 10.3 online). By contrast, *estimated* reliabilities in the online sample tended to equal or exceed those of on-campus courses when class size was equated. The four exceptions to this pattern were items 4, 5, 10, and 11. Ratings of these items achieved greater stability with fewer raters in on-campus classes than in online classes. Item 5 (relative grade) was particularly problematic; the observed inter-rater reliability was .31 online (versus .74 on campus), and it was estimated that thirty-five raters would be needed for a reliability of .70. Notice, however, that in the online sample, fewer students on average responded to this item than to other items (7.0 for item 5 versus 10.6 for all other items).

Item Clusters. Principal components factor analyses with Varimax rotation were conducted separately for the on-campus and online ratings data and yielded the same results for each data set. In each case, there were three factors with eigenvalues (characteristic roots) greater than 1: items 1 through 4 (global evaluation), items 6 through 9 (relative effort), and items 10 and 11 (hours spent). Item 5 failed to load on any factor and thus was excluded from further analysis. Based on the results from the other ten items, UW researchers computed an aggregate score for each of the three sets of items for each student rater and then calculated class-level

Table 4.2. Observed and Estimated Inter-Rater Reliabilities of Eleven Student-Rating Items by Class Mode

Items	Mean number of raters per class	Observed reliability	Estimated reliability for number of raters			
			7	10	15	20
1. Course as a whole						
On campus	20.8	.89	.73	.79	.85	.88
Online	10.8	.86	.80	.85	.89	.92
2. Course content						
On campus	20.7	.86	.68	.75	.82	.86
Online	10.8	.82	.75	.81	.87	.90
3. Instructor's contribution to course						
On campus	20.7	.90	.75	.81	.87	.90
Online	10.8	.81	.74	.80	.86	.89
4. Instructor's delivery format effectiveness						
On campus	20.7	.90	.76	.82	.87	.90
Online	9.8	.66	.58	.67	.75	.80
5. Expected grade relative to other course						
On campus	19.7	.74	.50	.59	.68	.74
Online	7.0	.31	.31	.40	.50	.57
6. Relative intellectual challenge						
On campus	19.7	.80	.58	.67	.75	.80
Online	10.6	.75	.66	.74	.81	.85
7. Relative effort in course						
On campus	19.6	.77	.54	.62	.71	.77
Online	10.7	.74	.65	.72	.80	.84
8. Relative effort to succeed						
On campus	19.6	.78	.56	.65	.73	.78
Online	10.6	.72	.63	.71	.79	.83
9. Relative involvement in course						
On campus	19.7	.68	.43	.52	.62	.68
Online	10.6	.63	.52	.61	.70	.76
10. Average hours per week						
On campus	19.5	.91	.79	.84	.89	.91
Online	10.7	.68	.58	.66	.75	.81
11. Valuable coursework hours per week						
On campus	19.6	.88	.72	.78	.85	.88
Online	10.6	.65	.55	.64	.73	.78

reliabilities for the aggregates. Figures 4.1 through 4.3 show the estimated reliabilities (using Spearman-Brown) of the three aggregates for various numbers of raters by course type. The global evaluation curves were similar across the two modalities but not identical, due to the lower reliability of item 4 in the online setting (Figure 4.1). The greatest similarity across modalities was found for the relative effort mean. As shown in Figure 4.2, the curves were essentially the same. Finally, as suggested by the results presented above for the individual items, the hours-worked mean was much more stable with far fewer raters in on-campus classes than in online classes (Figure 4.3).

Figure 4.1. Estimated Reliabilities of the Mean of Items 1 Through 4 (Global Evaluation)

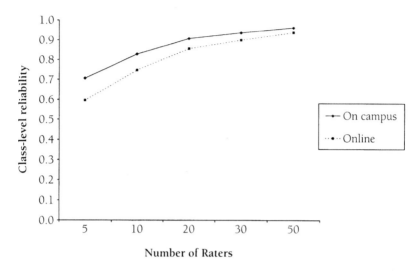

Note: Abridged text of the items: 1, Course as a whole; 2, Course content; 3, Instructor's contribution to the course; and 4, Instructor- or delivery-format effectiveness. The class-level reliability refers to the intraclass correlation coefficient.

Figure 4.2. Estimated Reliabilities of the Mean of Items 6 Through 9 (Relative Effort)

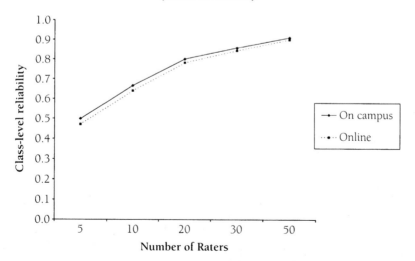

Note: Abridged text of the items: 6, Relative intellectual challenge presented; 7, Relative effort in the course; 8, Relative effort to succeed; 9, Relative involvement in the course.

Figure 4.3. Estimated Reliabilities of the Mean of Items 10 and 11 (Hours Spent)

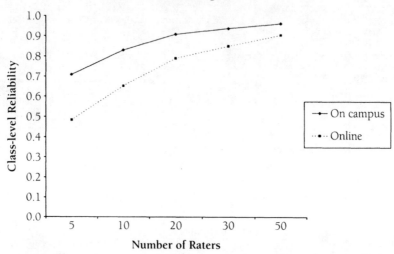

Note: Abridged text of the items: 10, Average hours per week (spent on course); and 11, Valuable course-work hours per week. The class-level reliability refers to the intraclass correlation coefficient.

Discussion

Overall, the reliability of IAS student ratings tends to be high and fairly comparable for both ratings of distance courses obtained through the Web and on-campus courses obtained in the classroom. Most items showed adequate inter-rater agreement when there were fifteen students or more rating the class. However, because online classes often have fewer students per class, the *actual* reliability of the ratings in any particular class may be lower than expected or desired. For example, for item 5 (relative expected grade) the "average" on-campus instructor with twenty students could reasonably assume that the mean rating is a reliable indicator of student opinion. A peer who taught an online class of ten students would likely not be as confident in the aggregate because the reliability for ratings on item 5 in online classes with ten student raters has been estimated to be .40.

Much can be learned from examining the items on which on-campus and online classes differed. For example, students in online classes had much greater diversity of opinion regarding the effectiveness of the online delivery format than their on-campus peers had about their instructors' teaching effectiveness (item 4). Considering the relative newness of online technologies, however, this finding is perhaps not so surprising. In addition, students in online classes reported a wider range in their estimates of time spent on a course than did their on-campus counterparts (cluster 3).

Such findings, along with the observation that the relative-grade item (item 5) was less reliable in online classes, suggest that there may be a sizable student effect in online courses that is not present to the same degree in traditional, on-campus courses. One possible explanation for this is that students in online classes are simply more diverse than those in on-campus classes. Another is that there may be some subset of students who find online classes particularly difficult or taxing. The lower *relative-grade* average in online courses, coupled with higher mean ratings on items assessing relative effort, tends to support this supposition.

However, results were more similar between modes than they were different. That is, for both formats the summative-evaluation items (1 through 3) evinced greater reliability than the relative-effort items (5 through 9). In addition, similar factor structures were extracted from the on-campus and online data. This is important for two reasons. First, it suggests that the item sets transfer well over course and rating modalities. Second, from a practical standpoint, the aggregate of items 1 through 4 are routinely included in IAS and IAS Online course-summary reports, but this practice is based on previous analyses of on-campus course data only. This study provided empirical evidence that this aggregate is appropriate for summaries of online course ratings (although a warning about the lower reliability of item 4 may be in order).

Finally, it would be instructive to execute an experimental design in which, in addition to the standard practice of distance courses being rated online and classroom courses being rated on paper forms, some on-campus student ratings are collected through IAS Online and some online course ratings are collected by paper and pencil. Only then will we be able truly to disentangle the effects of mode of instruction and mode of data collection.

Conclusion

The pattern of results observed in this study tends to mirror the results from other studies of online student ratings compared with classroom student ratings (for example, Waschull, 2001). The results are also similar to examinations of the psychometrics of psychological questionnaire data collected by the Web (for example, Buchanan and Smith, 1999). That is, online students reported more effort but gave overall evaluations similar to their classroom counterparts; and the inter-rater reliabilities and underlying scale structures of data obtained by the two modalities were comparable. As such, it would seem that differences observed in the present study of online and paper-based systems were more likely due to differences in instructional formats and student populations than to ratings modality.

References

Buchanan, T., and Smith, J. L. "Using the Internet for Psychological Research: Personality Testing on the World Wide Web." *British Journal of Psychology*, 1999, *90*, 125–144.

Cohen, P. A. "Student Ratings of Instruction and Student Achievement: A Meta-Analysis of Multi-Section Validity Studies." *Review of Educational Research,* 1981, *51,* 281–309.

d'Appollonia, S., and Abrami, P. C. "Navigating Student Ratings of Instruction." *American Psychologist,* 1997, *52,* 1198–1208.

Feldman, K. A. "The Association Between Student Ratings of Specific Instructional Dimensions and Student Achievement: Refining and Extending the Synthesis of Data from Multisection Validity Studies." *Research in Higher Education,* 1989, *30,* 583–645.

Gillmore, G. M. "Drawing Inferences About Instructors: The Inter-Class Reliability of Student Ratings of Instruction." *OEA Reports,* 2000, no. 00–2. Office of Educational Assessment, Washington University. [http://www.washington.edu/oea/0002.htm]. Access date: Aug. 25, 2003.

Green, K. C. "Campus Computing 2001: The 12th National Survey of Computing and Information Technology in U.S. Higher Education." Paper presented at the EDU-CAUSE Annual Conference, Indianapolis, Oct. 29, 2001.

Greenwald, A. G., and Gillmore, G. M. "No Pain, No Gain? The Importance of Measuring Course Workload in Student Ratings of Instruction." *Journal of Educational Psychology,* 1997, *89,* 743–751.

Kane, M. T., Gillmore, G. M., and Crooks, T. J. "Student Evaluations of Teaching: The Generalizability of Class Means." *Journal of Educational Measurement,* 1976, *13,* 171–183.

Knight, J., Ridley, D. R., and Davies, E. "Assessment of Student Academic Achievement in Online Programs." Paper presented at the 38th Annual Forum of the Association for Institutional Research, Minneapolis, May 1998.

Lewis, L., Snow, K., Farris, E., and Levin, D. "Distance Education at Postsecondary Institutions: 1997–98." Washington, D.C.: National Center for Education Statistics, U.S. Department of Education, 1999, NCES 2000–013.

Lowell, N., and Gillmore, G. M. "Reliability of the Items of the Instructional Assessment System: Forms A-G." *OEA Reports,* 1991, no. 91–1. Office of Educational Assessment, Washington University.

Marsh, H. W., and Roche, L. A. "Making Student Evaluations of Teaching Effectiveness Effective: The Critical Issues of Validity, Bias, and Utility." *American Psychologist,* 1997, *52,* 1187–1197.

Pasveer, K. A., and Ellard, J. H. "The Making of a Personality Inventory: Help from the WWW." *Behavior Research Methods, Instruments, and Computers,* 1998, *30,* 309–313.

Spooner, F., Jordan, L, Algozzine, B., and Spooner, M. "Student Ratings of Instruction in Distance Learning and on-Campus Classes." *Journal of Educational Research,* 1999, *92,* 132–140.

Stanton, J. M. "An Empirical Assessment of Data Collection Using the Internet." *Personnel Psychology,* 1998, *51,* 709–725.

Waschull, S. B. "The Online Delivery of Psychology Courses: Attrition, Performance, and Evaluation." *Computers in Teaching,* 2001, *28,* 143–147.

DEBBIE E. MCGHEE *is a research scientist for the Office of Educational Assessment at the University of Washington in Seattle.*

NANA LOWELL *is the director of the Office of Educational Assessment at the University of Washington in Seattle.*

5

Achieving adequate response rates can be a challenge for online student-rating systems. In this chapter, online-rating response rates and ways they can be improved are examined.

Online Student Ratings: Will Students Respond?

Trav D. Johnson

Student ratings of instruction are the most common means of evaluating teaching at U.S. colleges and universities (Glassick, Huber, and Maeroff, 1997; Seldin, 1999). Student ratings have been administered almost exclusively during class time using paper-pencil questionnaires—a costly, time-consuming process that is inconvenient for faculty and often restricts the thoughtfulness and depth of student responses.

The increasing use of technology in education, especially the World Wide Web, has led to the development of online administration and reporting of student ratings. In a survey of the two hundred "most wired colleges" in the United States, 25 percent of respondents said they were already using or were planning to convert to online student ratings (Hmieleski, 2000). A Web search (Clark, 2003) to discover institutions using online evaluations yielded more than sixty universities using online student ratings for some courses (for example, specific colleges or departments, distance-education courses) and eleven universities using online ratings for their entire campuses. Hoffman (Chapter Two in this volume) found that 10 percent (about twenty-five) of the respondents in his sample used online ratings as the primary means of collecting student-rating data on their campuses.

Online student ratings have many potential benefits, including ease of administration; more complete data collection; longer, more thoughtful student responses; reduced processing time and costs; more accurate data collection and reporting; and more detailed, user-friendly reports. There are also some major obstacles to successful implementation of online ratings, most notably, that of obtaining adequate response rates.

NEW DIRECTIONS FOR TEACHING AND LEARNING, no. 96, Winter 2003 © Wiley Periodicals, Inc.

Response Rates for Online Ratings

Unlike traditional paper-pencil student ratings that are administered in class, online ratings are usually completed outside of class during students' discretionary time. This allows students more time to fill out the rating forms, but it also gives them more freedom in their decision of whether or not to complete the forms.

Many institutions—the University of Colorado, Duke University, Georgia Institute of Technology, the Air Force Academy, Kansas State University, Northwestern University, and the University of Idaho—have identified response rate as a challenge to online ratings (based on Web searches conducted February 2002 and June 2003). Universities using online ratings have implemented a number of strategies to increase response rates. For example, some universities ask teachers to simply encourage their students to complete the forms. Another common strategy is to help students understand the importance of their input and how student-rating results are used. Georgia Institute of Technology provides detailed information to students and faculty about the online rating system and its use. Northwestern University provides student-rating results to students. Incentives are offered at some universities. Polytechnic University in New York enters participating students in a drawing for handheld computers. Murdoch University in Perth, Western Australia, sends students multiple e-mail reminders and enters participants in a drawing for a cash prize.

Studies of Response Rates at Brigham Young University

Brigham Young University (BYU) is a large private Doctoral/Research-Extensive University with over 32,000 students. At BYU, the first centrally administered student ratings began in the 1950s. Development of the current online student-rating system began in the late 1990s.

Obtaining adequate response rates has been a primary issue in the development and implementation of online student ratings at BYU. Concerns about response rates contributed to a particularly long period for testing and implementing the online system (over five years). To address these concerns, BYU launched several studies to examine online response rates, analyze response rates under different conditions, and determine how response rates can be improved.

The first pilot of online student ratings at BYU was conducted during winter semester 1997. This pilot included thirty-six courses and yielded a response rate of about 40 percent. The second pilot, conducted in 1999, included 194 course sections and 8,285 students. This pilot yielded a response rate of 51 percent. As part of the second pilot, online and paper rating forms were compared in seventy-four course sections. For these seventy-four sections, the response rate was 50 percent for online ratings compared with 71 percent for the paper-pencil ratings. A third pilot was conducted in fall 2000, which included forty-seven course sections and 3,076 students. For that semester, the response rate was 62 percent.

In winter 2002, a final pilot was conducted using a stratified random sample of course sections in departments across campus (that is, 10 percent of course sections from each of the sixty campus departments). For this pilot, identifying course sections and communicating with the appropriate instructors and students for the selected sections proved problematic. Some instructors and students did not receive information about their participation in the pilot study; many students were perplexed when asked to complete paper and online ratings for the same course; sometimes it was unclear to instructors and students which courses were part of the study and which were not. This confusion seemed to contribute to the low response rate for this pilot: about 30 percent. Because of the problems associated with this pilot, its low response rate was not considered an accurate predictor for online-rating response rates in future semesters.

Based on a number of factors, including results from pilots conducted before winter 2002, the BYU administration decided to move forward with campuswide implementation of online student ratings. Beginning in fall 2002, online ratings were available for all BYU courses, although individual instructors or departments could choose to use the old paper rating forms for their courses. Most of the campus used the online questionnaires, although a few departments and individual instructors chose to use the paper rating forms for their courses. The response rate for the entire campus was 58 percent. During winter semester 2003, the campuswide response rate increased to 60 pecent. (Note that calculations of response rates for these two semesters included instructors or courses that chose not to use the online student ratings because there was no way to identify and separate nonparticipating instructors or courses from those that were participating in the online ratings.)

Possible Reasons for Increase in Response Rates over Time

Data collected from faculty and students at BYU suggest several factors that may increase response rates for online student ratings, including the following: student access to computers, amount and quality of communication to teachers and students regarding the online rating system, communication to students regarding how student ratings are used, and faculty and student support of the online rating system. These factors generally increased over the time during which online ratings were piloted and fully implemented at BYU (from 1997 to 2003).

Student access to computers has steadily increased since the first online rating pilot in 1997. Most BYU students have their own computers. Some colleges on campus have recently required all their majors to own laptop computers. The number of computers in computer labs and the number of computer labs have also increased.

E-mail communication to faculty and students about the new online rating system became more frequent with each pilot and was standardized during campuswide implementation. Steps were taken over time to increase the clarity of the communication. Also, some evidence indicates that in the later pilots and campuswide implementation, a greater percentage of participating faculty and students actually received and read the messages about the online ratings that were sent by e-mail.

In addition to e-mail communication, the online student ratings were publicized through campus posters and newspaper advertisements during campuswide implementation. These posters and newspaper advertisements ran throughout the student-rating periods of the fall 2002 and winter 2003 semesters.

Some recent efforts have helped students understand how rating results are used. For example, e-mails to students contain brief information on the importance of student ratings and the uses of rating results. More extensive information on these topics is included on a student Web site devoted to online student ratings. Information has also been shared with students through meetings with student government. Although this is a good start, more needs to be done to help students understand the purposes and uses of online student ratings (for example, presentations during new-student orientation and working more closely with campus student government and other student groups).

There are some indications that faculty and students have grown more supportive of online student ratings at BYU. Recent student surveys and focus groups have indicated high levels of support for online ratings. Faculty support is more guarded but also is increasing. In addition, the communication from faculty members to students about online ratings has increased. More faculty members encouraged or assigned students to complete the forms in the later pilot studies.

Response Rates Under Various Conditions

Faculty members participating in the third pilot (fall 2000) were asked to report on their communication to students regarding completion of the online rating forms. Seventeen (50 percent) of the thirty-four participating faculty members reported what they told students. Their communication to students is categorized as follows:

Instructors assigned students to complete the online student-rating form and gave students points for completing the assignment (seven instructors).
Instructors assigned students to complete the online student-rating form but did not give points for completing the assignment (four instructors).

Table 5.1. Response Rate by Communication Category

Communication	Response rate, %
Assigned students to complete online rating forms and gave them points for doing so	87 (range: 59 to 95)
Assigned students to complete online rating forms but did not give them points	77 (range: 31 to 10)
Encouraged students to complete the online forms but did not make it a formal assignment	32% (range: 17 to 41)
Did not mention the online student-rating forms to students	20 (range: 8 to 42)

Note: Average response rates across classes in this category are not weighted according to number of students in each class.

Instructors encouraged students to complete the online rating form but did not make it a formal assignment (four instructors).

Instructors did not mention the online student-rating form to students (two instructors).

Table 5.1 shows the categories of faculty communication to students with the student-rating response rates in each category.

When faculty members assigned students to complete the online rating forms (whether or not points for the assignment were given), response rates greatly increased. It is not clear why there was such a wide range of response rates in each of the communication categories.

Response Rate and Length of Student Rating Forms

Three different forms (long, eighteen items; medium, ten items; and short, six items) were used in the third pilot study. Different forms were used to determine the amount of time students took to complete different lengths of forms and to see if the time it took to complete the forms made a difference in the response rate. The average time it took to complete one long form for one class was three minutes five seconds. The average time to complete one medium form for one class was two minutes eighteen seconds. The average time to complete one short form for one class was two minutes twenty-nine seconds. The average time it took students to complete forms for all their courses (using different combinations of short, medium, and long forms) was thirteen minutes forty-seven seconds. (Note: Responses taking more than half an hour for individual forms and taking more than one hour for all forms were removed when calculating means. These few responses were obvious outliers and likely occurred when students did things other than complete the forms during the time when the rating screen was open.)

Nearly all students in the focus groups agreed that the length of the rating forms was not a factor in their decisions to complete the forms (that is, the forms were quick to complete online regardless of the different lengths of the forms).

Students Completing Rating Forms for All Their Courses

Some faculty members and administrators at BYU assumed that if students accessed the online system to rate one of their courses, they would go ahead and rate all their courses. This was not necessarily the case. In the third pilot, data were collected on the number of students who completed rating forms for all their courses. Of the 1,892 pilot students who completed forms for at least one of their courses, only 638 (34 percent) completed forms for all their courses.

Even though the percentage of students rating all their courses was low, pilot results showed that students who had more than one course included in the pilot study were more likely to rate all their courses. Of the sixty-two responding students who were enrolled in two pilot courses, twenty-five (40 percent) completed questionnaires for all their courses. Of the thirty-eight responding students who were enrolled in three pilot courses, twenty-eight (74 percent) completed questionnaires for all their courses. It appears that when completion of online rating forms is assigned or encouraged in more than one course (as was the case in most of the pilot courses), the likelihood of student respondents completing questionnaires for all their courses improves considerably.

Response Rate for Open-Ended Comments

Of the 17,279 rating forms completed in the third pilot, 10,943 (63 percent) included written student comments. This is far more than the number of forms containing written comments using the paper, in-class rating system (less than 10 percent of the paper forms include written comments). In addition, the length of the written comments for online rating forms was greater than the length of comments when using the paper system.

Students completing the short form were more likely to make written comments. On the short form, 71 percent of responding students made written comments compared with 63 percent on the long form and 61 percent on the medium form. This is more than five times as many comments as students typically made on the paper rating forms.

Why Some Students Did Not Respond

In a telephone survey of nonrespondents (those in the pilot study who did not complete online rating forms), students were asked why they did not complete the online rating forms. Twenty-five students were contacted. Of these twenty-five students, eleven said they were aware that one or more of their courses was included in the pilot study. Of these eleven students, four said they had completed the online rating forms, six said they did not complete the forms, and one could not remember if she or he completed the forms or not. The six students who did not complete rating forms were asked why they did not complete them. Four of the six students said they forgot. The remaining two students said they did not complete the online forms because they were required to complete paper-pencil forms in class, and the online forms were optional. It is unclear why fourteen of the twenty-five students were not aware of their classes' participation in the pilot study.

Possible Bias When Response Rates Are Low

Both faculty and students at BYU have expressed concern that low response rates may cause a negative bias in student rating results. The hypothesis is that students who are upset or disappointed in a course or with an instructor are more likely to complete online rating forms. Therefore, a low response rate would yield a negative bias in overall ratings. To test this hypothesis, both online and paper-pencil rating forms were administered in seventy-four course sections.

Web-Paper Correlation. The correlations between the online and the paper rating results were .84 (overall instructor) and .86 (overall course). On the average, the overall course and instructor ratings were 0.1 point *higher* using the online rating system than they were using the paper system. For fifty (68 percent) of the sections, the average online rating was the same or higher than the paper rating for the overall instructor and overall course items. The remaining twenty-four (32 percent) of the course sections had overall instructor and course ratings within 0.1 to 0.5 points of the paper rating (on a seven-point scale). There is no evidence that lower response rates on the online ratings resulted in lower rating scores.

Correlation Between Rating Means and Response Rates. For the paper rating form, six (8 percent) of the sections had a response rate of less than 40 percent. The lowest response rate was 13 percent. For the paper form, the correlation between response rates and the overall ratings was 0.41 for both overall instructor and overall course items. This correlation accounted for about 17 percent of the variance in the rating results. It appears that the higher the percentage of attendance on the day the *paper* form was administered, the better the overall ratings.

For the online ratings, 13 (18 percent) of the sections had less than a 40 percent response rate. The lowest response rate was 33 percent. The correlations between response rates and overall ratings were 0.09 (overall instructor) and 0.10 (overall course). If a low Web-response rate biased the results, there would have been a much higher correlation between overall rating results and response rates. Results from this study suggest that online student ratings are much less susceptible to response-rate bias than paper-pencil student ratings.

Strategies to Increase Response Rates

Faculty members responding to a survey identified low response rates as an obstacle to successful online ratings. Only two made comments about remedies. One faculty member suggested that completion of the online forms should be a homework assignment. Another faculty member was concerned that students might resent having to complete the rating forms as assignments.

Students participating in the third pilot expressed some concern about achieving adequate response rates using online ratings. When asked, students also provided a number of suggestions to increase response rates (student comments are listed in order of frequency with the most frequent comment first):

Withhold students' early access to grades until they log on to the online rating system. This would be effective and not too restrictive (nearly all students in the focus groups supported this approach).

Provide extra credit or points for those who complete the forms.

Provide education and instructions regarding the online rating system.

Encourage instructors to show a personal interest in students completing the rating forms (for example, instructors could mention the evaluations in class, let students know that they pay attention to student responses, and send personal e-mails to students reminding them to complete the forms).

Provide positive incentives (for example, contribute money to a charity for each form completed, give students free coupons for food or for the campus bookstore for completing the forms).

Provide greater student access to computers.

Response Rates for Campuswide Online Student Ratings

For the first two semesters of campuswide implementation of the online ratings, response rates were 58 percent and 60 percent, respectively. These percentages included all BYU courses, even though one college and some departments and individual instructors did not participate in the online rating system (in other words, they explicitly told students not to complete online ratings for their courses because they were using other rating forms for the course). All courses were included in calculating percentages because the current online rating system does not provide a means to remove nonparticipating courses from the database. Therefore, if only those courses actually participating in the online ratings were included, the overall response rates would be above 60 percent for the two semesters.

During the semesters that online ratings were implemented campuswide, faculty were given the names of students who completed ratings for their courses (when at least five students completed ratings for a given course). These names were provided to faculty members only so they could encourage students who had not completed the ratings to do so. (To help ensure confidentiality of responses, student identification was kept in a separate database from rating results and never connected in any way to students' responses.) Faculty could also have paper forms administered on the last day of class to students who had not yet completed the online ratings. Data from the online and paper forms were merged when reporting rating results. In addition, some instructors gave students extra credit for completing the online rating forms. These strategies seemed to help increase response rates.

Even though response rates appeared to be enhanced by providing instructors the names of students who completed rating forms for each course, this practice has met some resistance. Notwithstanding the measures taken to preserve student confidentiality, some students are concerned that faculty will be able to use the names in some way to determine which students provided which responses on the rating forms. Some faculty and administrators question the practice of giving extra points to students for completing online forms. Providing instructors with names of students completing rating forms does not necessarily result in instructors' awarding extra points, but it does encourage the practice.

Discussion

Findings from the BYU studies help answer three primary questions about response rates and online student ratings: What contributes to low response rates for online ratings? Do low response rates bias results? How can response rates for online ratings be increased?

What Contributes to Low Response Rates for Online Ratings? Research was conducted to see if the length of the online student rating form affected response rates. Forms containing eighteen, ten, and six items were tested. The length of the form did not appear to be an important factor in students' decisions to complete the forms, although there would undoubtedly be a threshold at some point. If eighteen items were not too many, how many items *are* too many? At what point would response rates be significantly influenced? What factors affect the response rate in relation to the number of items on the rating form? In the future, faculty, chairs, and deans will be able to add items to the BYU online rating form. Research on response rates when items are added to the form may help answer these questions.

Do Low Response Rates Bias Results? It is interesting that response rates for online ratings were *not* negatively biased, even when response rates were relatively low. Apparently, students who are dissatisfied with a course are not more likely than other students to respond to online ratings. Or at least, dissatisfied students are not more likely to respond than students who are satisfied with the course (that is, only the very positive and very negative students could be responding, resulting in a mean similar to that of the whole class).

Further research is needed on levels of response rates and online ratings. Can the results of the BYU study be replicated and generalized? If low online response rates have little effect on course rating means, can low response rates be accepted as valid? What might explain the lack of correlation between response rates and online rating results (0.09 to 0.10), especially compared with paper-pencil ratings where there is a significant correlation between response rates and course student-rating means (0.41)? Answers to these questions may help determine how, and to what extent, online student ratings are used in the future.

How Can Response Rates for Online Student Ratings Be Increased? Research on student ratings suggests that an important factor in response rates is students' belief that rating results are used for important decisions about courses and faculty (Ballantyne, 1999). Results of the BYU studies support this finding. Many students commented on the importance of faculty members using the student-rating results. Some were adamant, almost demanding, in their insistence that faculty members see and pay attention to what they said in the open-ended comments. Students wanted to be heard and to know that their responses make a difference. When students believe this is the case, many are motivated to complete the online rating forms.

It was surprising how many students supported withholding early access to grades for those who had not completed the online student-rating forms (or withholding early access to grades to those who had not at least logged on to the online rating system). Students said that this strategy would be effective and yet not too restrictive.

Faculty members assigning students to complete the online rating forms had a considerable effect on response rates. This was true whether or not points were given for the assignment, albeit response rates were generally the highest when points were given. Why was the mere assignment to complete the forms so effective, even in classes where points were not given? One hypothesis might be that students thought their participation in online ratings might affect their standing in the course regardless of whether points were actually given for the assignment. Or, making the ratings an "assignment" may have motivated students to complete the forms because of the message this sent that completing the forms was important to the faculty member (that is, if instructors care enough to make it an assignment, maybe they also pay attention to and use the results).

Conclusion

At BYU, response rates are the primary concern about online student ratings of instruction. Research has revealed a number of strategies that may be effective in increasing response rates, including the following: student access to computers, communication to faculty and students regarding the online rating system, communication to students about the uses of rating results, and faculty and student support of the online rating system. Efforts to address these areas have generally resulted in increased response rates. Current online response rates at BYU are approaching 70 percent. Strategies used to increase response rates at BYU may be useful to other institutions that are using, or are considering the initiation of, online student ratings.

References

Ballantyne, C. "Improving University Teaching: Responding to Feedback from Students." In Zepke, N., Knight, M., Leach, L., and Viskovic, A. (eds.), *Adult Learning Cultures: Challenges and Choices in Times of Change.* Wellington, Australia: WP Press, 1999, pp. 155–165.

Clark, S. J. *Use of Online Student Ratings at Institutions of Higher Education: Results of a Web Search.* Provo, Utah: Faculty Center, Brigham Young University, 2003.

Glassick, C. E., Huber, M. T., and Maeroff, G. I. *Scholarship Assessed: Evaluation of the Professoriate.* San Francisco: Jossey-Bass, 1997.

Hmieleski, K. *Barriers to Online Evaluation: Surveying the Nation's Top 200 Most Wired Colleges.* Troy, N.Y.: Interactive and Distance Education Assessment Laboratory, Rensselaer Polytechnic Institute, 2000 (Unpublished Report).

Seldin, P. "Current Practices—Good and Bad—Nationally." In P. Seldin (ed.), *Changing Practices in Evaluating Teaching: A Practical Guide to Improved Faculty Performance and Promotion/Tenure Decisions.* Bolton, Mass.: Anker, 1999.

TRAV D. JOHNSON is a faculty development coordinator over instructional evaluation and teaching assistant training at the Faculty Center at Brigham Young University, Provo, Utah.

In this chapter, the author examines important issues related to online reporting of student survey results.

Online Reporting of Results for Online Student Ratings

Donna C. Llewellyn

With the introduction of online course surveys comes the related issue of reporting survey results. This chapter is based on the experiences of Georgia Institute of Technology in Atlanta (hereafter, Georgia Tech), a large, Doctoral/Research-Extensive institution where all end-of-term course surveys have been online since the fall semester of 1999. This chapter presents ideas about online reporting of student ratings of instruction, and the main benefits of and concerns with such a system are addressed.

Background

In the fall of 1999, Georgia Tech implemented an online course-instructor survey system. The existing paper-pencil course-instructor survey system was converted to a Web-based system; in making this conversion, only the process changed (paper and pencil to online), leaving the rating-form content and design unaltered. This transition to online ratings of instruction was undertaken for several reasons: a change in the academic calendar from quarters to semesters, the retirement of the old mainframe computer that had housed the formats for the old paper survey form, and a growing dissatisfaction with the delays inherent in getting reports out using a manual system.

The paper survey was originally designed and implemented in 1986. It was administered during the last two weeks of the quarter in every class with at least seven enrolled students. The creation of the survey and the compilation of the results were automated, and all interaction with the survey

NEW DIRECTIONS FOR TEACHING AND LEARNING, no. 96, Winter 2003 © Wiley Periodicals, Inc.

system was done through the Web. The transition to an electronic survey initially changed only a few features of the procedure. The actual survey content was kept exactly the same, and the survey was still made available only during the last two weeks of classes.

Because the surveys are now generated automatically, they are tied to an instructor-class combination (rather than being tied solely to the course). This enables multiple instructors of a particular class to each be rated individually. Furthermore, the academic unit can decide whether a course will be surveyed, instead of size being the only determining factor. In addition, in the fall of 2001 the survey was shortened. In the spring of 2003, the survey period was extended through finals week.

The current survey is organized into five parts. Every student-rating form contains ten core questions (called the *institute core questions*). Each department can add up to three optional questions taken from a question bank of about two hundred questions. Each instructor then has the option of adding up to three additional questions from the same question bank. Finally, there are two sections for open-ended student comments—one directed to the instructor about the course and her or his teaching, and the other directed to the office that administers the survey (for the purpose of gaining feedback about the online survey process).

The original survey had a core of twenty-four questions; the departments could add up to five questions, and the instructor could add up to seven questions. The only change that has occurred in the content of the survey since it was put on the Web is that it has been shortened, primarily with the intent of decreasing the time required to complete it. The push for this change came from faculty. Because the survey is now done on students' own time rather than during a class session, many faculty members wanted the process to be as efficient and brief as possible; they assumed that a shorter form would encourage more students to complete the surveys.

Logistics of Online Reporting

The reports in the survey system are "hard-coded"—that is, users are not able to define their own reports. Initially, three standard reports were built into the course survey system. For the faculty members, there was the usual report for a single instructor-course combination in a particular semester. For administrators, there were two reports: one provided the results for a collection of courses (specified by a range of course numbers) within a specific academic unit during a particular semester, and the other provided the results for a collection of courses for a specific instructor from a number of semesters. In response to requests from users, two additional reports were created after the system went online. One is the "cross-listed course report" and the other is the "item 24 report."

At Georgia Tech, there are many cross-listed courses. For a cross-listed course, there might appear to be several different courses with the same identification number taught by the same professor but offered by several different departments (for example, Civil and Environmental Engineering 1770 and Mechanical Engineering 1770). In reality, all students who register for these various courses end up in the same classroom taking the same class. Because the surveys are generated by course identification number (which includes the name of the offering department), different surveys and reports are generated for each of the listings of this same course. Initially, each report presented only the results and statistics of those students who registered for that particular listing of the course. The faculty members who teach cross-listed courses asked that a summary report be created that combines all of the individual reports (and hence calculates the statistics for the whole class rather than only its departmental portions). This is known as the "cross-listed report."

The final item on the course-instructor opinion survey is "The instructor is an effective teacher" (rated on a five-point Likert scale). This item is used as the main indicator of teaching effectiveness at Georgia Tech. For many years, this item was known as "item 24" because of its placement as the twenty-fourth item in the paper survey. Although it is now the tenth item on the online survey, it is still known by its old moniker. Using this item, administrators compare instructor performance in their academic units. To assist them, the "item 24 report" was created, which gives only the results for this item for a collection of courses within an academic unit during a specific semester.

Students were concerned about instructors having access to the survey results before grades were submitted. Therefore, to ensure that there is no interference between course survey results and grades, the instructors are not given access to the reports until after final grades are submitted.

To allow the faculty to see their own results before the administration does, the reports generated for administrators are not available until the seventh day of the following semester. These administrators' reports omit the comments section, and for units higher than the immediate department or school, they also omit the schools' optional items.

The reports are available to the appropriate persons through any Web browser from any computer with access to the Internet. When an instructor logs on to the system, there is an authentication process that checks an identification number and password to verify that the user is indeed an instructor. Faculty members have access to only their own reports. A school chair has access to the reports for all of the courses within her or his school. Likewise, the deans have access to all reports for all courses within their colleges. The reports can be saved to the user's computer; they can also be printed directly from the browser.

The standard online instructor report looks exactly like the paper reports that were produced under the previous system. This consistency in format was maintained to ease the transition from the old paper system to the new online system. A sample report (Exhibit 6.1) is provided here.

Exhibit 6.1. A Sample of Online Report Results for Single Course-Instructor Report

Student Survey Response Report
For Fall 2001 course: ISYE1000A—Industrial and System Engineering
Instructor: Smith, Nosuchperson CRN: 87654 Class Size: 25 Final Survey
Core Questions

Item	(5) Strongly Agree	Agree	Partly Agree and Partly Disagree	Disagree	(1) Strongly Disagree	Not Applicable	Number of Respondents	Interpolated Median
1. Course seemed well planned and organized	13	10	1	0	0	0	24	4.6
2. Good job covering course objectives and content	14	10	0	0	0	0	24	4.6
3. Explained complex material clearly	13	11	0	0	0	0	24	4.6
4. Was approachable and willing to assist	16	5	3	0	0	0	24	4.8
5. Encouraged students to consult with him or her	14	9	1	0	0	0	24	4.6
6. Class attendance important in promoting learning of material	12	11	1	0	0	0	24	4.5
7. Number of assignments was reasonable	6	13	4	0	0	0	23	4.1
8. Exams covered course content and objectives	7	14	3	0	0	0	24	4.1
9. Exams were of appropriate difficulty	4	18	2	0	0	0	24	4.1
10. The instructor was an effective teacher	14	10	0	0	0	0	24	4.6

Student comments about the class or instructor

The best instructor I ever had! Give her a raise.

This was an interesting class and the professor was always prepared and organized. I will recommend her to all of my friends.

I can't believe they let this person teach here—fire her!

Sometimes the material seemed rushed and was hard to learn. And the tests were way too long. But the prof. was really nice!

Thanks for caring about the students—wish there were more here like you.

Benefits of Online Reporting

Reporting course-survey results electronically has many benefits. First, specialized reports requested by academic units are fairly easy to program and make available to users. Currently the student-ratings survey and all of the related reports at Georgia Tech are programmed in ColdFusion (a product of Macromedia). This is an HTML-like language used for creating dynamic, data-driven Web pages.

At the present time, the Georgia Tech programming staff is considering a change to Crystal Reports (a product of Crystal Decisions), a powerful Windows-based tool for writing database reports. Many people at Georgia Tech know how to create customized reports using Crystal Reports. In addition, Crystal Reports can be stored in a central repository to be downloaded and used or changed as desired. (Indeed, this process is used frequently for other administrative reports on campus—for example, to generate transcripts, missing grade reports, and dean's list candidates.) Taking this approach would be more efficient than requiring a specialized computer programmer to design a new (hard-coded) report through ColdFusion, and it would allow maximum flexibility in the types of reports generated.

Because reports are now available through the Internet, faculty no longer have to be on campus to access their reports. Moreover, if they misplace their own reports (or if they neglected to print them in the first place), they can always access them again as needed. (See "Concerns Related to Online Reporting" later in this chapter for a caveat to this benefit.)

The online-system data are now also more accessible to other individuals. Researchers investigating correlations related to student ratings can now easily access the rating data for analysis. (For example, researchers may want to look at whether the course level or the particular college offering a course affects student perceptions of the course.)

In addition, all students now have online access to the results of the core items. The students previously had their own system, called "the course critique," which published the statistical results from two of the items on the course-instructor survey. When the online survey instrument was shortened in 2001, the faculty senate approved a measure to merge the two systems. Now students can access statistical results for all ten core questions for any course that has at least five responses and a response rate of at least 30 percent. Students have always relied on the course critique to explore faculty-course combinations before registering for classes each term. This student reliance on the evaluation results is a motivator for their participation in the online surveys, which provide data for the new online critique system.

Many larger departments at Georgia Tech analyze the differences in course-survey results from different types of classes and from the various sections of the same course. In the past, this required entering all of the data from the printed reports into a spreadsheet program. Now, because the data are presented electronically, they can be saved directly into a spreadsheet program. This eliminates a time-consuming task that was often fraught with errors.

Perhaps the most important benefit of online reporting is that the reports are available almost immediately. This timeliness of the new system contrasts sharply with the former process, which often took up to six weeks to distribute the paper reports to the academic units. This online advantage allows better use of the results by faculty members for improving their teaching. With the online system, instructors can fine-tune their courses during the following semester, whereas with the paper system, the delay in receiving reports meant that teachers were often unable to react to the results and make changes until two terms later.

Concerns Related to Online Reporting

Some concerns have surfaced regarding access to electronic survey reports. The administration is most concerned about the issue of compliance with open-records legislation. If one central office has access to electronic survey results, those results are available to anyone who chooses to file an open-records request. In fact, several such requests have already been made on limited scales.

However, related to this issue is another question: because no paper copies of reports are distributed to the faculty, at what point can a centralized office feel secure in deleting electronic files? Faculty commonly either forget to print their results (even though they are advised to do so), lose their copies, or even forget that they are available. In addition, although most departments print a complete set of reports for their unit every semester, this task is sometimes also neglected in some departments. Moreover, faculty members are required to include certain results in their promotion and tenure vitae. Therefore, no matter how much this issue is publicized, some faculty members will be adversely affected by a wholesale purging of the reporting database.

The current policy is to maintain indefinitely the results of the core items (those common to all surveys) and to purge all optional items and student comments after about three years. In this way, the results that are needed for promotion, tenure, and post-tenure reviews are always available. However, the parts of the survey that are specifically intended only for the instructor's own formative evaluation will not be available for public scrutiny after three years. Because the usefulness of formative data decreases over time, data older than three years would be of little value.

Another concern with online course surveys is the anonymity of student responses. In the Georgia Tech online-evaluation system, the student responses are kept without any identifying information. The student identification number and a list of the surveys she or he has completed are kept in separate databases. For about two minutes after a completed survey is submitted, there is a connection between the survey results and the student identification number. (This ensures that a student cannot simultaneously log into the system on multiple computers and submit multiple surveys for a course.) This connection is dissolved after the information from the survey has been submitted and the database is updated. After that point, it is physically and technically impossible to connect a student's identification number with her or his survey results. In fact, this system is more secure than the previous paper-pencil system, when it was possible to identify students by their handwriting.

Unresolved Issues and Questions

Now that results of the course surveys are easily accessible, questions arise about who should have access to the online database. At present, researchers have access to the data without faculty and student identifiers. What, if any, restrictions should be placed on this access if these researchers are current students at Georgia Tech? In addition, should the central administration have access to *all* results? Unit administrators currently have access to the core results of their unit; however, no administrators have access to the open-ended comments, and administrators above the deans have access to only those results that are available to students. For what purposes, if any, should these restrictions be relaxed?

Another important consideration has to do with the appearance of the online system. What format and design of reports is most useful for online student ratings? Should reports include links to other online resources that are directly related to the results of the surveys? Georgia Tech has perhaps erred on the side of caution by retaining the format of the old survey reports; more study is needed to find out if another format would work better in the new online environment. Another related concern is that some faculty members are still uncomfortable reading instructions and printing pages from the Web. For these individuals, the best format seems to be any format that can be easily printed by someone else and placed in a campus envelope.

Finally, when an instructor accesses a report, a header states that it is an "unofficial report" because the same person who is reviewed in the survey is now viewing it. However, at this time, there is no such thing as an "official" report (although when an administrator accesses a report, the "unofficial report" header is not there). This situation raises the issue of whether self-printed versions of the online reports are valid for portfolios. Furthermore, will those outside the institution accept these unofficial reports, or do they need to be certified in some way as official?

One of the problems with being at the forefront of a new process is that there are more questions than answers. Georgia Tech is committed to the online process for student surveys and faculty reports. Ongoing research, discussion, and refinement will make the online evaluation system more viable and effective.

DONNA C. LLEWELLYN is director of the Center for the Enhancement of Teaching and Learning at Georgia Institute of Technology in Atlanta.

7

In this chapter, the authors compare the costs of online student ratings of instruction with those of paper-based systems.

Do Online Ratings of Instruction Make $ense?

Timothy W. Bothell, Tom Henderson

This chapter provides a case study comparing the costs of online student ratings of instruction with those of traditional paper-pencil student ratings. The case study is derived from Brigham Young University's (BYU) experience in creating and implementing a new online student rating system. Some of the information on costs was supplemented by data gathered at Washington State University in Pullman.

The chapter is organized into five sections: background information about the case study; a description of the costs categories used in the costs comparison; the actual costs and estimates of costs; the comparison of costs of the paper-pencil system with the costs of the online system; and finally, other issues to consider when comparing online with paper-based evaluations.

Importance of the Costs Comparisons

The growing use of technology in higher education raises many questions about the possible cost savings of using an online rating system. The costs comparisons explored in this article cannot be considered analyses of "cost-effectiveness" because only costs-to-costs are compared. An analysis of cost-effectiveness is beyond the scope of this study.

Using technology to administer questionnaires can cost less than administering questionnaires by traditional means. In this study, technology plays an important role in reducing costs. Data collection, tabulation, and analysis are activities that computers can do more quickly, more accurately, and for lower costs than people completing these same tasks. (See "Personnel Time Expended in Processing Paper-Based Surveys" in this chapter for an example of time spent for human data entry and analysis of a paper-based college survey.)

Related Research

Some researchers have suggested that faculty prefer paper-pencil evaluations of teaching (Dommeyer, Baum, Chapman, and Hanna, 2002), primarily because faculty members tend to believe that the paper-pencil questionnaires will produce more responses and higher ratings than online methods. In contrast, some administrators may favor online systems (if the accuracy and response rates of the two systems are similar) because they tend to assume that online systems reduce costs.

In Hmieleski and Champagne's (2000) survey of the nation's two hundred "most wired colleges," 22 percent of the institutions conducted a costs analysis of paper-based evaluations. Ten schools reported costs that ranged from $0.25 to $4.00 per student-rating form. These researchers attributed the wide range in costs to the factors used to calculate costs. Their explanation was that "low cost estimates are usually based solely on the costs of evaluation forms, while high cost estimates usually account for many of the 'hidden' costs of evaluation (for example, labor costs to photocopy, count, collate, and deliver forms; and to retrieve, scan, store, and deliver results to stakeholders)" (p. 1). The accuracy of a comparison of costs-to-costs is questionable if all related costs are not included.

Kronholm, Wisher, Curnow, and Poker (1999) provided a more detailed analysis of the costs of Web-based evaluations. They compared the costs of production, distribution, monitoring, scanning, and analysis for both paper- and Web-based evaluations of a distance-learning course. They found that a twenty-two-item paper-based questionnaire cost $1.74 per student evaluation (assuming labor costs of $15 per hour). They reported that the same twenty-two-item questionnaire administered online cost $0.06 per student evaluation. Their paper-based costs were in the middle of the range identified by Hmieleski and Champagne (2000). Kronholm, Wisher, Curnow, and Poker (1999) also compared costs between paper- and Web-based questionnaires. They reported a cost savings of nearly 97 percent when using Web-based questionnaires instead of paper-based questionnaires.

Few studies address the costs of student ratings of instruction. What is clear from these few available studies is that reports of costs can vary widely depending on the cost categories included and the processes used to collect data. This chapter provides a set of cost categories for comparing the costs of paper-pencil and online evaluations that can serve as a model for other institutions involved in similar research.

Student Ratings of Instruction at BYU

BYU, operated by the Church of Jesus Christ of Latter-Day Saints, is a large private Doctoral/Research-Extensive university in the western United States (Provo, Utah). With an enrollment of about 30,000 students, it offers bachelor's, master's, and doctoral degrees.

At BYU, paper-based student ratings of instruction began in the 1950s. At that time, classes were randomly selected for evaluation. Paper-pencil evaluations were administered near the end of the semester during class time.

In 1995, the university participated in its once-a-decade reaccreditation by the North Central Association of Colleges and Schools. In preparation for reaccreditation, the university engaged in extensive self-studies. An outcome of the process was the recommendation that a new student-rating questionnaire be developed. Another was to provide evaluation of every course by every student every semester for little or no increase in costs. In short, the self-study called for a new evaluation system and the doubling of service without a major increase in resources. Online student ratings were deemed an effective way to meet this challenge.

In the fall of 1996, a university-wide committee of faculty, administrators, students, and technology staff began work to develop the new online student-rating system. Since that time, committees, task forces, and councils have continued work on this project through 2003.

To lay the groundwork for cost comparisons of the online and paper systems, Wood (1997) analyzed costs for the paper questionnaires in 1997; he estimated that it cost the university about $0.23 to process one questionnaire and report the results back to the instructor.

Then, in the fall of 1998, a milestone in the development of online student ratings occurred when the university initiated a program wherein all students and faculty would have access to the Web and to e-mail. At that point, the prospect of using a Web-based rating system became more feasible. Several versions of the evaluation questionnaires and a number of approaches to online evaluation were piloted over subsequent years. As part of the ongoing development process for the online evaluations, research was conducted to compare and contrast the differences between using paper-pencil and online questionnaires.

By the summer of 2000, the project gained momentum through the collaboration of individuals from several campus units: central administration, Testing Services, Office of Information Technology, and the Faculty Center (the campus faculty and instructional development unit). They piloted the new online ratings system, solicited feedback, researched specific issues, and recommended changes. Most faculty, administrators, and students surveyed supported the new system (Johnson, 2000). By the fall of 2002, the university had implemented a systematic process for collecting and reporting online ratings of instruction campus-wide for every class and every teacher.

From this brief history of student ratings of instruction at BYU, it is clear that development is one of the major costs in initiating online student ratings of instruction. Development costs can span several years and include a large amount of time spent educating faculty, staff, and students about online evaluations. These and other costs are detailed below.

Costs Categories

In comparing paper-pencil and online student ratings, BYU researchers examined three major costs categories: development costs, operating expenses, and miscellaneous costs.

Development Costs. Development costs include time spent in consultation and meetings, education about the data collection methods and procedures, research, design, computer programming, and coordinators' management of the development project. For this study, all salary and wages for employees' time were assigned monetary values by using average salary figures (for the respective time periods when the development occurred) plus 34 percent of salary for benefits (for example, health insurance, retirement). Development costs also included the purchase of equipment, software, and hardware.

Operating Expenses. Operating expenses include the costs of all materials (for example, paper, envelopes, labels, and data connection lines) plus employee time to assist in distributing, administering, and collecting forms. Operating expenses also include salary and wages for delivering evaluation forms, administering forms to students, collecting forms, scanning evaluation forms, inputting data, tabulating data, and creating and delivering reports. Again, all full-time personnel labor was given monetary values by using average salary figures plus 34 percent of salary for benefits.

Miscellaneous Costs. Miscellaneous costs include expenditures that are difficult to quantify and those that do not fit neatly into the categories of development or operating expenses. An example is the cost incurred when users choose to print paper copies of their Web-based student-rating reports. The paper printouts of the reports are not a requisite part of the operating costs for the online system, yet they are a cost that the university incurs.

Actual and Estimated Costs

Tables 7.1 and 7.2 detail the costs for the paper-based and online ratings systems for BYU's student ratings of instruction. Actual costs were obtained from records; other costs were estimated by the people involved in the process. All costs for salaries, materials, and the like were calculated according to the dollar value at the time the costs were incurred. In addition, all costs

Table 7.1. Costs of BYU Paper-Based Student Ratings of Instruction

Cost Category	Cost Item	Cost Description	Annual Costs, $
Development Total costs = $133,964, prorated over 20 years = $6,698 per year	Salary and wages (average salary per hour plus benefits at the time of development)	Personnel time spent on research, designing materials, coordinating and managing the evaluation project, promoting and educating others about student ratings, and miscellaneous meetings (9 months of full-time work spread across several years for each of five faculty [$12.50 an hour], 10 hours each for three administrators [$17.50 an hour], 40 hours for one supervisor [$10 an hour], 480 hours for two graduate students [$5 an hour]) Total cost = $125,714 ($418,460[a])	6,286 (prorated) 20,923[a]
	Scanning machine	Scanning machine and software to run scanning machine: total cost = $8,250	$412.50 (prorated) the same[a]
Operating expenses in 2002 Total costs = $415,503 per year	Paper and printing costs	Paper rating forms: one sheet, double-sided; $0.095 per sheet; 400,000 paper student rating forms per year Paper reports: one sheet, double-sided; $0.095 per sheet; 24,500 sections One per section rated:	40,328 5,635 784 11,520
	Envelopes	24,500 sections rated each year, $0.23 per envelope One per envelope:	
	Labels	24,500 envelopes per year, $0.032 per label	
	Scanning and report preparation	Processing of 400,000 paper rating forms per year, including data input and preparing reports: equivalent of 40 hours each for six students ($8 an hour); scanner runs for 800 hours at about 500 sheets an hour	
	Class time	University incurs "lost opportunity" costs to administer paper rating forms in class; these consist of teaching time lost while administering paper rating forms during class: 20 minutes per class; 24,500 classes per year 8,167 hours of faculty time (Average estimated faculty salary per hour + benefits in 2002 = $43.33) 353,876	
	Distribution and collection of forms	Department secretaries, teaching assistants and other staff who administer and collect paper rating forms: estimated 4 hours each for fifty people ($16 per hour, $3,200); testing center student employees: 10 hours each for two students ($8 an hour), $160	3,360
		Total Cost	422,201 (436,838[a])
		Cost per Student Rating Form	$1.06 (roughly $1.09 in 2002)
		Derived from total costs divided by total number of paper student-rating forms per year	

Notes: Faculty salaries calculated using data from the Higher Education Research Institute Faculty Survey 1998–1999 (for BYU faculty).
[a]Roughly the cost in 2002.

Table 7.2. Costs for BYU Online Student Ratings of Instruction

Cost Category	Cost Item	Cost Description	Annual Costs, $
Development Total costs $813,394, prorated over 10 years $81,339 per year	Salary and wages (average salary per hour plus benefits in 2002)	Personnel time spent on research, designing materials, developing the online process, coordinating and managing evaluation project, promoting and educating others about online ratings, miscellaneous meetings (12 months of full-time work spread across several years for each of five faculty* [$41.88 an hour], 5 months for one administrator [$48.32 an hour]; equivalent of two and a half years of full-time work for one project manager [$35.43 an hour], 480 hours for one graduate student [$14 an hour], 80 hours for one graduate student [$14 an hour]; 1 hour for each of 800 faculty proximately one-half the faculty at the University] for department meetings to orient faculty to the online system [$43.33 an hour]): total cost = 718,280	71,828 (prorated)
	Software and hardware	New software for online data collection ($4,462) and two network servers ($5,000): total = 9,462	946 (prorated)
	Programming	Personnel time to write computer code for online system (6 months each for two full-time programmers [$29 an hour]): total 60,320	6,032 (prorated)
	Paper-based supplements during pilot period	Paper-based version of the online student-rating form used to increase response rates in some classes during the pilot period. Paper supplement costs were estimated to be 6 percent of the yearly total paper-based costs found in Table 7.1 (6 percent of total = 25,332)	2,533 (prorated)
Operating expenses Total costs = $101,218 per year	System management	Management of online system database: equivalent of one month full-time work for one manager ($29 per hour)	4,640
	Network use	Annual fee for access to network line: Office of Information Technology ($450 per year)	450
	Classroom time	University incurred "lost opportunity" costs by using class time to encourage students to complete the online rating forms; these consist of teaching time lost while encouraging students to complete online rating forms: 5 minutes per class; 24,500 class sections per year 2,042 hours of faculty time (Average estimated faculty salary* per hour + benefits in 2002 = $43.33)	88,479
	Promoting new online system	Publicity campaign to educate faculty and students and to encourage participation (campus posters, newspaper ads)	7,648
Miscellaneous Costs Total costs = $4,060 per year	Web software	The online student-rating system uses university-licensed software, estimated 2 percent of $200,000 annual university licensure fee	4,000
	Paper printouts of reports	Some teachers and administrators print paper copies of the Web-based reports, estimated 2,000 one-page reports ($0.03 per page)	60
		Total Cost	186,617
		Cost per Student	$0.47

(Derived from total cost divided by total number of online student-rating forms per year)

*Faculty salaries calculated using data from the Higher Education Research Institute Faculty Survey 1998–1999 (for BYU faculty).

were calculated as if all students evaluated all courses and all instructors. Although not all students submitted evaluations, performing the calculations as if they did provides an estimate of what the upper limit of costs would be. The same number of students was used in calculations for both the paper costs and the online costs. Development costs for each evaluation system were prorated over the expected life of the system to obtain an annual value of development costs. This annual value for development was used in the calculation of total costs. The total annual costs were then divided by the total number of student-rating forms per year to obtain the cost per student-rating form.

A large percentage of the costs for the paper-based forms comes from class time used to administer the questionnaires. These costs are regarded as "lost-opportunity" costs because they represent time taken away from teaching. Much less class time is used in the Web-based system because instructors merely explain the online evaluation process and encourage students to complete the forms online.

Costs Comparison

This section looks at three important issues involved in comparing the costs of student ratings of instruction: development costs, prorating strategy of the rating system, and annual operating costs.

Development Costs. The development costs reported in this study are the actual costs at the time of development. The rough equivalencies for 2002 dollar amounts are also provided for the development costs of the paper-based system.

Prorating Strategy. Another issue with implications for development costs is the system's expected life cycle—the time from development until the time of obsolescence or redevelopment. Although the paper-based system has evolved over more than forty years, the current paper system was substantially redesigned about twenty years ago. Hence, in this study, the life cycle of the paper-based system is twenty years. Consequently, the development costs were prorated over this twenty-year period.

The expected life cycle for the current Web-based system is less than that for the paper-based system due to the rapid rate of change in technology. For this reason, the development costs for the online system were prorated over only ten years—half the expected life cycle of the paper system. This shorter prorating period doubled the calculated costs per year for developing the online system.

The development costs for the Web-based system were about twelve times more than for the paper-based system (after prorating development costs for both systems). Part of this difference is due to the higher wages of employees developing the Web-based system over the past five years compared with those who developed the paper-based system twenty years ago. The difference is also due to the time spent to develop the two systems. The total time estimated for development of the paper system was 7,750 hours compared with 16,560 hours for the online system. Thus, the estimated hours spent on the Web-based system development were more than double those spent for development of the paper system.

Annual Operating Costs. The annual operating costs of the two systems also differ. The total estimated operating costs for the paper-based system were $415,503 per year, about four times the estimated operating costs for the Web-based system, which were $101,218. For the online system, these calculations include the miscellaneous operating costs of university-licensed Web software and paper printouts of the Web-based reports. Even with these miscellaneous inclusions, there is a substantial savings in operating the online system. Much of the salary and wages spent operating the paper-based system are eliminated in the online system. The greatest saving realized by the online system is the reduction of time spent in class administering the evaluations.

One way to make a cost comparison is to calculate the estimated cost of each student-rating form (that is, by dividing the total cost by the total number of student-rating forms). In this study, the estimated cost for the paper-based system was $1.06 per student-rating form (see Table 7.1). For the online system, the estimated cost was $0.47 per student-rating form (see Table 7.2). Therefore, the use of technology to collect student ratings of instruction can result in a savings of over 50 percent compared with the paper-based system. In one year, the Web-based system at BYU saves about $235,000. Three areas account for the most savings within the online system: decreasing the time taken away from classroom teaching; reduction in printing costs; and reducing personnel time and other costs of data collection, processing, and reporting.

Personnel Time Expended in Processing Paper-Based Surveys

Washington State University (WSU) analyzed personnel time expended in the processing of paper-based surveys. Washington State is a public Doctoral/Research-Extensive university with its main campus in Pullman and other campuses in Spokane, Vancouver, and Tri-Cities. WSU has approximately 22,000 undergraduate and graduate students. The WSU study analyzed the number of hours spent on data entry for 156 paper-based surveys that were mailed to alumni of the WSU College of Veterinary Medicine. Every five years, the veterinary college surveys its alumni from the five previous graduating classes; the survey results are used for curricular improvement and accountability.

The surveys were formatted and printed using a word-processing program. (Scannable surveys were considered but were not used due to the length of the two surveys, the cost involved in the custom formatting of scannable forms, and time constraints.) The WSU survey administrators spent about ninety-five hours in the following activities: building a database (using Microsoft Access) and testing data input (forty hours); double-entering the responses into the database (thirty-one hours); and finally, checking for errors and correcting discrepancies (twenty-four hours). Each survey response was entered into the database twice, each time by a different person. The two entries were then compared, and when the answers did not agree, the numbered survey was retrieved and the corrected answer entered into the database. Researchers then double-checked a small sample of responses for the accuracy of the data entry.

The ninety-five hours expended in survey processing would be more than cut in half if an online system were used to collect the data. This simple example from WSU suggests a need to decrease personnel time spent in processing surveys; this personnel time could be substantially reduced through the use of online surveys.

Other Issues Beyond Costs

When considering the merits of paper versus online systems, the costs are important. But cost is not the only issue. The costs for Web-based questionnaires may be less than half of the costs for paper-based questionnaires; nevertheless, these cost factors should be evaluated in light of several other issues, including response rate, versatility, nonresponse bias, and access and appearance of the questionnaire.

Response Rates. The response rate for student evaluations is an important issue when comparing paper-based and online systems. Some campuses have experienced lower response rates when changing from paper to online questionnaires (for example, Johnson, 2002). On the other hand, by using incentives, Yale University experienced a high response rate when initiating online student ratings (Sullivan, 2003). For an in-depth analysis of response rates, see Chapter Five in this volume.

Versatility. The online accessibility of ratings and reports is one advantage of an online system. In addition, Web-based forms are easily modified, including for use in midcourse evaluation (Henderson, 2001; Lieberman, Bowers, and Moore, 2001). Web-based forms are also useful for online and distance-education courses. These features make the online form attractive to faculty and administrators. An online system is also attractive to students because of its "anytime-anyplace" convenience. Paper-based systems lack this degree of versatility and accessibility.

Nonresponse Bias. Nonresponse bias or nonresponse error occurs when some people, or members of a demographic group, are less likely to respond to a survey than others—for example, illiterate people would be unlikely to respond to a written survey (Salant and Dillman, 1994). Some research suggests that compared with women, men respond at a higher rate to online surveys than to paper surveys (Palmquist and Stueve, 1996; Tomsic, Hendel, and Matross, 2000). If men continue to respond at a higher rate on Web-based surveys, it would appear that online surveys have a non-response bias against women.

A more recent national survey of college students, "Assessing Response Rates and Non-Response Rates in Web and Paper Surveys," indicated that women respond at a much higher rate than men on both paper and online surveys (Sax, Gilmartin, and Bryant, 2003). If this is the case, paper and online surveys both have similar nonresponse biases against men (in other words, men are less likely to respond in either mode). More research is needed in this area; institutions of higher education should examine possible nonresponse biases in student ratings on their individual campuses.

Access and Appearance. Participants in an online ratings system undoubtedly have different computers, operating systems, types and sizes of screens, browsers, connection speed to the Internet, graphics cards, and so forth. Therefore, authors and administrators of an online system face a difficult challenge concerning the appearance of online components on participants' computer screens. To help meet this challenge, Dillman (2000) emphasizes the importance of designing for computer logic as well as questionnaire logic as a way to minimize errors in coverage, measurement, and nonresponse.

Conclusions

When comparing paper and online student ratings of instruction, three important cost categories should be considered: development costs, operating costs, and miscellaneous costs. To determine annual development costs, these costs must be prorated over the life cycle of the rating system. Because of the typically rapid changes in technology, the life cycle of an online system will likely be shorter than that of a paper system.

In the cost comparisons of student ratings at BYU, researchers found the following: First, overall, the online rating system costs about half what the paper rating system costs. The cost savings are primarily due to savings in three areas: less time taken away from classroom teaching, reduced printing costs, and reduced data-collection costs. Second, development costs are much higher for the online rating system than for the paper system. Third, operating costs are much higher for the paper rating system than for the online system. Finally, calculations of annual costs show that paper student ratings cost about $1.06 per rating form; online student ratings cost about $0.47 per rating form.

Costs are an important consideration when choosing a student-rating system; other factors should also be considered, including response rate, versatility, nonresponse bias, accessibility and appearance of the questionnaires. Once these and other factors are considered, online ratings become an viable option because of their cost benefits.

References

Dillman, D. A. *Mail and Internet Surveys: The Tailored Design Method.* 2nd ed. New York: Wiley, 2000.

Dommeyer, C. J., Baum, P., Chapman, K. S., and Hanna, R. W. "Attitudes of Business Faculty Towards Two Methods of Collecting Teaching Evaluations: Paper vs. Online." *Assessment and Evaluation in Higher Education,* 2002, 27(5), 455–462.

Henderson, T. "Classroom Assessment Techniques in Asynchronous Learning Networks." *Technology Source,* 2001. [http://horizon.unc.edu/TS/default.asp?show=article&id=908]. Access date: Aug. 26, 2003.

Hmieleski, K., and Champagne, M. "Plugging into Course Evaluation." *Technology Source—Assessment,* 2000. [http://horizon.unc.edu/TS/assessment/2000-09.asp]. Access date: Aug. 26, 2003.

Johnson, E. "Students Ignore Online Course Evaluations." *Daily Utah Chronicle,* Jan. 25, 2002. [http://www.dailyutahchronicle.com/main.cfm/include/%20detail/storyid/169755.html]. Access date: Aug. 26, 2003.

Johnson, T. *Summary Report: BYU Online Student Ratings.* Provo, Utah: Faculty Center, Brigham Young University, 2000 (Unpublished report).

Kronholm, E. A., Wisher, R. A., Curnow, C. K., and Poker, F. "The Transformation of a Distance Learning Training Enterprise to an Internet Base: From Advertising to Evaluation." Paper presented at the Northern Arizona University NAU/Web99 Conference, Flagstaff, Ariz., September 1999.

Lieberman, D. A., Bowers, N., and Moore, D. R. "Use of Electronic Tools to Enhance Student Evaluation Feedback. *Techniques and Strategies for Interpreting Student Evaluations.* New Directions for Teaching and Learning, no. 87. San Francisco, Jossey-Bass, 2001, pp. 45–54.

Palmquist, J., and Stueve, A. "Stay Plugged into New Opportunities." *Marketing Research: A Magazine of Management and Applications,* 1996, 8(1), 13–15.

Salant, P., and Dillman, D. A. *How to Conduct Your Own Survey.* New York: Wiley, 1994.

Sax, L. J., Gilmartin, S. K., and Bryant, A. N. "Assessing Response Rates and Nonresponse Bias in Web and Paper Surveys." *Research in Higher Education,* 2003, 44(4), 409–432.

Sullivan, W. "Online Course Evaluations Meet Early Success, Prof Says." *Yale Daily News,* Jan. 14, 2003. [http://www.yaledailynews.com/article.asp?AID=21224]. Access date: Aug. 26, 2003.

Tomsic, M. L., Hendel, D. D., and Matross, R. P. "A World-Wide Web Response to Student Satisfaction Surveys: Comparisons Using Paper and Internet Formats." Paper presented at the 40th Annual Meeting of the Association for Institutional Research, Cincinnati, May 21–24, 2000.

Wood, L. J. "Student Ratings of Faculty on the World Wide Web." Provo, Utah: Brigham Young University, 1997. (Unpublished paper.)

TIMOTHY W. BOTHELL is a faculty development coordinator for Assessment of Student Learning in the Faculty Center at Brigham Young University in Provo, Utah.

TOM HENDERSON is the assessment coordinator at the Center for Teaching, Learning, and Technology at Washington State University in Pullman.

8

*Course Evaluation on the Web is a dynamic, Web-based
system for student reflection on learning, instructor
reflection on teaching, and program management.*

Course Evaluation on the Web:
Facilitating Student and Teacher
Reflection to Improve Learning

Beatrice Tucker, Sue Jones, Leon Straker, Joan Cole

Excellence in teaching and learning is not easily achieved, and it requires
more than just a passing participation in an improvement activity (Weimer,
1990). To focus on achieving excellence, educational institutions must place
high value on both the process and the outcomes of teaching and evaluation.

Good-quality feedback on courses that informs instructors about student perceptions of their teaching is often difficult to obtain. Lack of
student feedback may leave instructors relying on their own perceptions
of teaching successes and difficulties, which may be different from student
perceptions. A cycle of evaluation and improvement based on student feedback is seen as essential to the process of quality improvement (Brown,
Race, and Smith, 1997). The improvement of teaching and learning is likely
when teachers are supported through a process of reflective dialogue based
on student feedback (Brockbank and McGill, 1998).

Traditional Feedback Systems

There are many methods of collecting course feedback. The traditional
paper-based method provides good quantitative and qualitative feedback,
but it is often time-consuming (for both students and teachers) and laborious to collate and interpret. Teachers who manage several courses often find

Note: Course Evaluation on the Web was funded by a Learning Effectiveness Alliance
Project awarded to the School of Physiotherapy from Curtin University of Technology.

it difficult to collate paper-based feedback in a timely manner—if at all—in order for the information to be useful in facilitating a change in teaching and learning practices.

Although traditional feedback systems generally focus on teaching performance, they neither recognize nor evaluate the student contribution to learning. Educators may have immediate access to student feedback using various course evaluation systems; however, there is typically no mechanism for reporting back to students about changes that may (or may not) occur. Students report frustration in spending time and effort to provide evaluative feedback when they see no apparent outcome.

A Broader View of Evaluation

Educators have an expectation of students' reflective practice, which implies that students have a responsibility for their own learning (Brockbank and McGill, 1998). Course content design can encourage some higher-order learning. However, transformative learning of relativist or constructed knowledge (Brockbank and McGill, 1998) can be facilitated by students reflecting on their own learning through participation in course review. Their participation helps students develop critical ability (Brockbank and McGill, 1998). In addition, they learn from observing the reflective practice modeled by teachers.

The School of Physiotherapy at Curtin University of Technology in Perth, Western Australia, recognizes that learning is influenced by many variables. Therefore, evaluation of teaching and learning should focus on changes in knowledge, skills, attitudes, and behavior. Figure 8.1 presents a model of the authors' understanding of the aspects that influence learning within a "learning community." This model suggests that student learning is a result of the interaction among several key elements: the students themselves, their student peers, the subject learning materials, and the faculty. The interaction is further influenced by ways these elements are managed and by the school's physical and social environment within the broader university and geocultural environment.

In 1999, physiotherapy faculty at Curtin University developed Course Evaluation on the Web (CEW, pronounced "cue"), a Web-based system that broadened the possibilities for effective evaluation within a learning community. CEW was initially piloted in one class with one hundred students. Since that time, CEW has been developed and used annually in sixty entry-level courses and twenty postgraduate courses. Five hundred students, fifty teachers, and ten program managers have participated in the CEW process.

The School of Physiotherapy uses CEW for student reflection on learning, instructor reflection on teaching, and administrator response to student feedback to improve programs. CEW is used to monitor student satisfaction with a variety of aspects of their educational experience. CEW is part of a

Figure 8.1. The Learning-Community Model

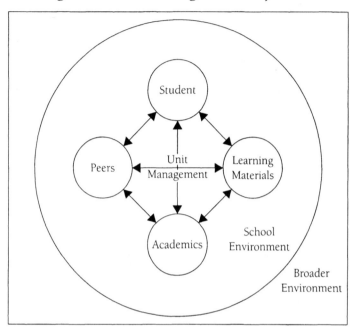

process of continuous quality improvement that involves the entire learn-ing community in order to enhance the quality of teaching and learning.

University programs need to demonstrate their accountability and are often audited by external agencies. As a result, they are required to demon-strate their quality improvement processes and to monitor their efficiency and effectiveness. It is essential to have a timely and efficient mechanism that responds to student feedback, facilitates course and program changes, and helps demonstrate accountability. Australian universities typically use the Graduate Careers Council of Australia Course Experience Questionnaire (CEQ) (http://www.gradlink.edu.au/gradlink/gcca/index.htm) to evaluate student satisfaction with their programs in the following areas of good teaching: clear goals and standards, appropriate workload and assessment, development of generic skills, and overall satisfaction. CEQ data are usu-ally received by schools nearly two years after a cohort has graduated, mak-ing it difficult to identify problem areas within courses or programs and to manage factors that affect student satisfaction. Waiting for CEQ scores until after students have graduated is untenable; this adversely affects recruitment and enrollment of both international and local students and, hence, the financial viability of programs.

Conversely, the CEW online system facilitates timely data collection, feedback, and evaluation using a Web-based interface. CEW provides the following benefits to students, teachers, and program administrators:

Students: CEW provides quick, anonymous feedback on the quality of courses or programs; it encourages students to reflect on their learning and to contribute to educational improvement.

Teachers: CEW provides rapid online access to student perceptions of their courses or programs; it encourages instructors to reflect on their teaching and to adopt the idea of continuous quality improvement.

Program administrators: CEW provides online access to a concise overview of student perceptions of the program, it encourages program administrators to identify areas where improvement is needed, it assists them in determining teacher development needs to improve teaching and learning and it provides information to determine appropriate resource allocation and to evaluate programs.

CEW Feedback Instrument

CEW incorporates all aspects of the learning-community model to evaluate teaching and learning. In the course and program-to-date instruments, students indicate their agreement with a variety of statements using a five-point Likert scale. Students respond to items in the following areas:

Students' own characteristics (for example, intellectual capacity, work and family responsibilities, knowledge)

Students' perceptions of their peers (for example, intellectual capacity, group dynamics)

Students' perceptions of their teachers (for example, knowledge, attitudes)

Course learning materials (for example, textbook, electronic resources)

Course management (for example, clarity of expectations, sequencing of material, type of assessments)

School environment (for example, physical facilities, psychosocial factors)

Broader environment (for example, university administrative efficiency, student support services, student's family and home, culture and lifestyle of the city).

In addition, qualitative data are collected from the following areas: best and poorest aspects of the course and program, suggestions for change, and other comments.

CEW Process

The CEW process consists of a Web-based feedback loop involving reflection and communication from students to teachers and administrators—and back again to students. Reflection is encouraged during and at the end of each semester by both students and teachers. A brief description of the main aspects of the CEW process follows.

A CEW management team consists of teacher and student representatives who meet regularly to review the instruments and mechanisms, negotiate participation with teachers and students, evaluate effectiveness, and implement changes as appropriate. Students agree to provide feedback as a compulsory course requirement. In exchange, teachers agree to inform students about changes that may be made as a direct result of student feedback. Student representatives actively encourage their peers to consider giving feedback on an ongoing basis and remind them of evaluation deadlines.

The CEW management team orients and teaches students, instructors, and program managers about the CEW system—its principles, goals, and functions. Professional development of both teachers and students is accomplished through the integration of formal teaching sessions and mentor support. A member of the CEW management team leads an educational session for new students on how to provide quality feedback.

Students and teachers have access to previous feedback and response reports about enhancements to teaching and learning through the closed community Web site. New teachers are mentored through their first use of the system by shadowing experienced teachers. The motivation for teacher and student participation in CEW is the belief that the process will result in improved teaching and learning. In recognition of the mutual benefits, teachers and students have made an ongoing commitment to use CEW to improve teaching and learning outcomes.

Each semester, student representatives of the CEW management team ask students to reflect on their learning at regular intervals (typically every two weeks). Students keep a record of their thoughts and comments on specific aspects of their programs using specially designed forms packaged as part of their learning materials. Teachers are also reminded regularly to reflect on their teaching and to record their thoughts in a course journal.

After their exams at the end of each semester, students are asked to provide online feedback on the subjects they studied and on their overall experience in the program to date. CEW delivers to students the appropriate feedback instruments, provides a password-protected interface for student feedback, and enables students to monitor feedback they have provided and feedback that is still required. The instruments for evaluating courses and programs are Web based, enabling students to provide their feedback from anyplace where they have access to the Internet. The identity of the respondents is encrypted to maintain student anonymity throughout the whole process.

The program-to-date feedback instrument measures the students' perceptions of their experiences to date in the School of Physiotherapy programs (Figure 8.2). It collects student ratings in the following areas: the school and broader environment, CEQ subscales, individual course satisfaction, and qualitative responses (for example, suggestions, other comments). From the items on the instrument, a score is automatically

Figure 8.2. The Course-to Date Interface

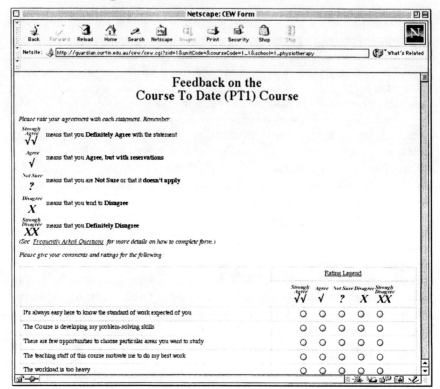

calculated for the following CEQ subscales of good teaching: emphasis on independence, clear goals and standards, appropriate assessment, generic skills, appropriate workload, and overall satisfaction.

Web-based student feedback provides results that are immediately available for processing and presentation to the respective teacher and administrator, who then begin the process of reflection. Because the students have agreed to provide feedback, a complete set of data is obtained. CEW conducts a frequency analysis on rating questions and generates a report with graphical representation of the distribution of rating scores on each question. Using key words, student comments are automatically sorted into appropriate categories to aid interpretation and analysis.

As part of the CEW process, teachers and program managers reflect on the ratings report, conduct further analysis on student comments, create a summary report of the student feedback, and prepare a response after discussion with a peer. This response provides an overview of the course, the teacher's perceptions of the best aspects of the course, and areas that require change. The teacher outlines whether he or she agrees with

Figure 8.2. (Continued) The Course-to Date Interface

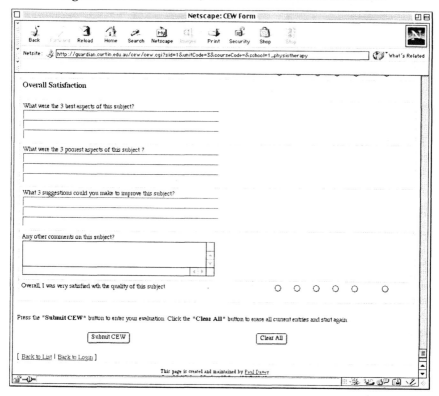

student perceptions and indicates which changes will (and will not) be made for the following year based on student feedback (and provides reasons for these decisions).

Once the summaries and draft responses are prepared, teachers discuss their feedback and proposed changes with a more experienced peer. This dialogue with peers is critical to the process of teacher reflection, and it is designed to be supportive, nonjudgmental, and nonthreatening. Instructors then share their ideas and proposed improvements with other teachers in the program. Such discussions include the following topics: strategies to improve teaching skills, evaluation strategies, development of appropriate resources, guidance in choosing appropriate teaching seminars within the university, and the opportunities for working with more experienced educators. The teacher and the more experienced peer then agree on the final changes that will be made to the course. This process focuses on peer mentoring and development to improve teaching skills; it is not simply a summative teacher review. Teachers value this opportunity to discuss ways to improve their teaching and their students' learning.

Closing the Feedback Loop

After the peer-review process, the course and program-to-date responses are communicated back to students. At that time, student representatives, teachers, and program managers review a summary of feedback, responses, and changes made as a direct result of student feedback in the subsequent semester. Copies of the ratings reports, summaries of student comments, and teacher and manager responses are posted to a secure learning-community Web site. On this Web site, students can see that their feedback has been heard and valued and that it has contributed to program improvements. Consequently, students maintain a high level of ongoing commitment to their role in the CEW process.

Benefits of Online Evaluation

There are many benefits of using an online evaluation system. Students, teachers, program managers, courses, and programs all benefit from the CEW process. Students have the opportunity to help improve their courses, teachers have accurate feedback to assist in improving their teaching, and program managers are able to identify excellent teaching and developmental needs to support the improvement of teaching. Finally, CEW provides an important mechanism for teacher accountability, including areas of student satisfaction with teaching and learning and evidence that course improvements are being made based on issues raised in the CEW process.

Student Reflection. CEW promotes improved student learning by engaging students in reflection during and at the end of each semester. Student perceptions of CEW have been evaluated by examining the quantitative and qualitative feedback provided by the CEW process. This includes the student representatives and also student focus groups comprising five to ten students in each year of each program (conducted by an external reviewer). After the first year of CEW implementation at the School of Physiotherapy, 63 percent of students reported that CEW encouraged them to reflect more on how they learned and how they were taught. Furthermore, 80 percent of students surveyed in 2000 believed that by giving feedback through CEW, they were improving the physiotherapy program.

Students highly valued the response reports they received about changes planned as a result of teachers receiving the students' feedback. They also said that CEW resulted in more discussion with teachers, especially about class content. Students also reported that the CEW process resulted in a more collaborative approach to learning and greater flexibility in teaching and learning (Student Survey 2000).

Teacher Reflection. During each semester, a report is circulated to all teachers that outlines student satisfaction with individual courses and provides a comparison with the previous year's data. This report provides instructors with the opportunity to review their own performance in a course. It also helps them see how their courses compare with other courses taught within the School of Physiotherapy. If teachers find that their course is performing poorly compared with other courses, they can identify teachers whose courses are performing well and seek their assistance in reviewing their own course structure and materials. They may choose to collaborate with those teachers to develop new teaching strategies. In this way, teachers can select their own mentors to help them improve their teaching and their students' learning.

Reflective teaching practice is an ongoing, cyclical endeavor that Weimer (1990) describes as "tinkering." To support this tinkering, the School of Physiotherapy saw the need for changes in culture, dialogue, and information. According to Ramsden (1998), the academics' environment profoundly affects their work processes, morale, and productivity. The School of Physiotherapy has tried to create an appropriate teaching culture through various initiatives, including monthly teaching seminars and small teaching development grants.

The teachers' perceptions of the reflective practice supported by CEW have been evaluated using focus groups and a Teacher Climate Survey. This survey was conducted in 2000 and again in 2002 by an external reviewer. Academics reported high levels of student focus and positive attitudes toward reflection, including a 50 percent increase in the time spent on reflection. Compared with the Teacher Climate Survey of 2000, academics reported higher levels of organizational support (through CEW) for reflective practice. The Survey of Perceived Organizational Support (Eisenberger, Fasolo, and Davis LaMastro, 1990) was used to measure organizational support. Scores on this survey increased from 3.8 in 2000 to 4.5 in 2002 (out of a possible score of 5.0).

CEW has also improved many aspects of teaching-related practice and organizational behavior. Job Motivational Potential (Cook, Hepworth, Wall, and Warr, 1981), which considers richness of work (related to job satisfaction, motivation, performance, absenteeism, and turnover), was examined over a two-year period. There was a 25 percent increase in job motivation potential to the point where work was considered well above the level where there would be opportunities for further increases in job motivation potential (Ots, 2002). There were similar significant increases in faculty job satisfaction, both intrinsically (12.5 percent) and extrinsically (28 percent), using a fifteen-item scale developed by Warr, Cook, and Wall (1979). Moreover, satisfaction with teaching improved by 30 percent despite a marked increase in teacher workloads. Organizational commitment also showed an improvement of 14 percent. All of these indicators demonstrate that an online evaluation system that supports teachers provides many additional organizational benefits.

The results of these studies are supported by statements such as these from teachers who used CEW:

CEW has had a major impact on the amount and quality of my reflection on my teaching. Having used the high-quality feedback students provide and benefited from the peer discussions, I cannot imagine teaching without CEW.

[Using CEW], "I feel we all talk a lot more about teaching and how we can improve our courses. I think it's given us a much more customer focus and is a powerful evaluation tool for new courses. It provides us with the evidence of what we do well and what we need to improve on and discussion of the strategies we might use to do this.

Mentoring and Developing Teachers. Critical to the success of CEW as a mentoring tool is the willingness of senior teachers, including the head of school, to share their own negative feedback and difficulties and their struggles for solutions. In this way, a high degree of trust and support is developed among teachers who have become more likely to expose their limitations and to receive support for finding new ways of improving their teaching.

Another catalyst used for mentoring teachers is the "CEW Expo" held at the end of each year. These expositions provide a forum for teachers to share their experiences about what has worked well and what has not worked well in their courses. For example, teachers describe a problem identified through CEW and how solutions emerged through personal reflection, discussion with students, and the peer-review process. Some teachers present problems and the proposed solutions. Others present the problems and the range of solutions they tried—but which have not worked—and seek the assistance of the wider group in solving the problems. In this way, teachers share a collective responsibility for improving teaching and learning, rather than the responsibility lying with a single individual.

Program Management. Several common themes for teacher development needs are identified through the individual and group peer-review process. When several teachers require the same assistance, workshops are organized to address these specific needs. Program managers generate a report that outlines student satisfaction and perception of workload with each subject in each semester of the program. This report enables program managers to identify subjects of concern and broad program weaknesses at a glance, to examine the strategies that have been identified for subject improvement, and to provide teachers with support as necessary.

Program managers not only compare courses at one point in time, they also see how particular courses change over time. Likewise, students and academics are able to review how the course changes from one year to the next. The trend in course and year feedback and performance is plotted over time across the CEQ subscales. This demonstrates whether changes implemented have resulted in improvements in student satisfaction with their programs. Areas that are rated poorly are easily identified, and strategies for improvement are implemented and then reevaluated.

CEW feedback provides teachers and program managers with a mechanism to monitor changes in student satisfaction well before program

Figure 8.3. Improvements in Teaching and Learning in Fourth-Year Bachelor of Science Physiotherapy Course, 2000 to 2002

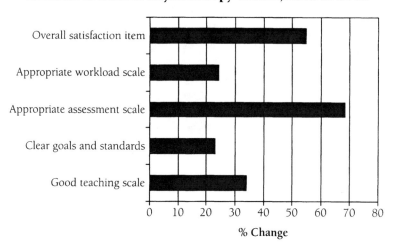

completion. Therefore, CEW is a powerful tool for predicting CEQ outcomes and the factors that are likely to affect program quality and satisfaction.

Through promoting reflection by students, teachers, and program managers, CEW has facilitated improvements in the quality of all areas of teaching and learning. For example, since 2000, the School of Physiotherapy has improved its scores in all fourth-year program-to-date ratings. Figure 8.3 shows the percentage improvements in CEQ-based teaching scales from 2000 to 2002. In 2000, the school experienced lower scores in appropriate assessment and workload. Based on this early warning, teachers and program managers worked on these areas in 2001. Their actions were deemed successful when subsequent scores improved in these areas and on the overall program satisfaction in 2002. When the 2000 graduate CEQ scores finally became available, there was indeed a drop in scores. Without CEW, this student dissatisfaction would not have been discovered until well after student graduation, which would have been too late to improve the program for those students then enrolled. In addition, CEW makes it possible for program managers to compare a school's performance with national averages or with other schools. This benchmarking function is valuable in the current competitive academic environment.

CEW also provides the School of Physiotherapy with data to measure against key performance indicators of success from the school, division, or university and the strategic planning framework in the areas of student satisfaction, improvement in delivery of products and services in teaching and learning, effective use of resources to achieve outcomes, and identifying teacher development needs to improve teaching and learning.

Conclusion

Based on a learning-community model, CEW is an effective tool to enhance reflective practice on teaching and learning. It also provides valuable benefits for continuous monitoring of teaching and learning in individual courses, across streams within programs, across whole programs, and between schools. Because CEW actively addresses student satisfaction and concerns, students commit to providing feedback within the learning community. Furthermore, the system is a mechanism to enhance program management, to improve student satisfaction, and to provide evidence of a quality-improvement process in educational programs.

Those thinking about educational course or program evaluation should consider an online evaluation tool as a way to solicit high-quality data in a timely manner. The success of such a system depends on the support of academics and the extent to which students participate and feel ownership of the process. Through CEW, the School of Physiotherapy at Curtin University has created a successful learning community committed to faculty-student reflection and educational excellence.

References

Brockbank, A., and McGill, I. *Facilitating Reflective Learning in Higher Education.* Bristol, England: Open University Press, 1998.

Brown, S., Race, P., and Smith, B. *500 Tips for Quality Enhancement in Universities and Colleges.* London, England: Kogan Page, 1997.

Cook, J. D., Hepworth, S. J., Wall, T. D., and Warr, P. *The Experience of Work.* London: Academic Press, 1981.

Eisenberger, R., Fasolo, P., and Davis LaMastro, V. "Perceived Organizational Support and Employee Diligence, Commitment and Innovation." *Journal of Applied Psychology,* 1990, *75,* 51–59.

Ots, J. *Employee Opinion Survey Report.* Perth, Western Australia: School of Physiotherapy, Curtin University of Technology, 2002.

Ramsden, P. *Learning to Lead in Higher Education.* New York: Routledge, 1998.

Warr, P., Cook, J., and Wall, T. "Scales for the Measurement of Some Work Attitudes and Aspects of Psychological Well-Being." *Journal of Occupational Psychology,* 1979, *52,* 129–148.

Weimer, M. *Improving College Teaching.* San Francisco: Jossey-Bass, 1990.

SUE JONES is a lecturer and coordinator in the School of Physiotherapy at Curtin University of Technology in Perth, Western Australia.

BEATRICE TUCKER is a lecturer and coordinator in the School of Physiotherapy at Curtin University of Technology in Perth, Western Australia.

LEON STRAKER is associate professor in the School of Physiotherapy at Curtin University of Technology in Perth, Western Australia.

JOAN COLE (recent head of school) is professor in the School of Physiotherapy at Curtin University of Technology in Perth, Western Australia.

Evaluation Online offers a variety of options to faculty who want to solicit formative feedback electronically. Researchers interviewed faculty who have used this system for midterm student evaluation.

Online Collection of Midterm Student Feedback

Cheryl Davis Bullock

The University of Illinois at Urbana-Champaign (UIUC) has experienced, as have many other institutions, an exponential increase in the number of courses offered online. The instructors of these online courses share the desire for, and in many cases the requirement of, a systematic process by which their students can provide feedback on their courses and teaching. At UIUC, the Division of Measurement and Evaluation (housed in the Office of Instructional Resources) oversees the traditional paper-pencil Instructor and Course Evaluation System (ICES). This division initiated the original concept, eventual development, and implementation of an online system to evaluate online courses and instructors. The development of this system was funded by the president's office. It is known as EON (for Evaluation ONLine) and has been available at UIUC since the summer semester of 2001.

One benefit of the new EON system is that it includes a mechanism for instructors to collect midterm (formative) feedback as well as end-of-term (summative) student ratings. In the traditional paper-pencil system, there was no mechanism for collecting and summarizing midterm student feedback. An online system for collecting and summarizing midterm student feedback has great value in higher education for a variety of reasons. First, it provides a snapshot of student perceptions about a course while course changes that semester are still possible. Consequently, the same students that provide the feedback can benefit from its implementation (Angelo and Cross, 1994). An added benefit of this mechanism within the EON system is that the results are immediately accessible once the evaluation period has ended. In addition, they are presented in a user-friendly format that can be easily summarized.

NEW DIRECTIONS FOR TEACHING AND LEARNING, no. 96, Winter 2003 © Wiley Periodicals, Inc.

This chapter focuses on midsemester online student evaluations for online courses and instructors. It briefly describes the EON system and then reviews the pertinent literature. The bulk of the chapter includes results from interviews with faculty using the online midsemester feedback system. The goal is to provide useful information about the midsemester online component for those teaching online and for those charged with facilitating the improvement of teaching and learning in higher education.

Review of the Literature

The first step in conducting the study was to identify areas within the literature to review. It was important to understand what makes a midterm evaluation system effective. Second, it was important to understand what, if anything, might be inherently different in collecting midterm feedback using an online system as opposed to a traditional paper-pencil system. It also seemed valuable to review the literature on future trends in collecting online midterm student feedback. The results from the literature on these topics are reviewed below.

Midterm evaluations, by the nature of their purpose and timing, are almost always formative (Scriven, 1967). Instructors typically use the results from formative, midterm student feedback solely for instructional improvement and rarely for inclusion in personnel documents (Overall and Marsh, 1979).

Student feedback has the potential to benefit the students who provide it (Kulik, 2001). Consequently, midterm results are most useful when received and interpreted in a timely manner. In addition, midterm evaluations include more open-ended questions than closed, or forced-choice, questions (Angelo and Cross, 1994).

One inherent element of paper-pencil feedback is that students' comments are handwritten. This can affect quantity and quality of student responses as well as the way the results are summarized and used. Compared with the paper system, the online system for midsemester feedback encourages students to write more and be more honest in their responses. Using an online system, students can type their responses rather than handwrite them. Because they are typing their comments, they are likely to include more information in response to each item than if they were handwriting their responses (Ballantyne, 2000). Furthermore, with the online system, students who lack understanding of a course concept can make this known to an instructor without revealing their identity through their handwriting (Sheehan, 2001). In addition, the timeliness of online systems allows instructors to receive midterm feedback quickly and respond to it in class the next day.

EON System

The UIUC has a strong tradition of the institutionalized use of student ratings. The student-rating system, typically called ICES, has been in place at UIUC since 1976. About six thousand courses per semester—taught by faculty, nontenured instructors, and teaching assistants—administer ICES to collect student feedback. Twelve outside institutions also use ICES for student evaluation of instruction. Originally developed for formative evaluation, ICES also plays an important role in summative evaluation (for example, promotion, tenure, and merit increases).

EON grew out of the ICES system to provide an online system for evaluating online courses. Until the EON system became available, online instructors who wanted or needed to collect student ratings would often mail paper-pencil ICES forms to their online students. These online students were asked to complete the paper forms and mail them to the central administrative office, which they often neglected to do. In addition, there was no institutional mechanism for collecting midterm feedback from online students. Now, for the first time, EON not only meets the end-of-course needs of online students and instructors, it provides the means to collect midterm data in a centralized system.

Brief Description of the EON System. The EON system allows instructors to create student feedback forms that are part of a university-wide system. It permits students to securely log in and complete these forms, using their unique UIUC identification and password. Using the EON system, instructors develop evaluation forms, students complete these forms, and instructors receive the results. With instructors' permission, administrators may also view the results. EON was designed as a "smart system" in that it sends reminders to appropriate users at appropriate times. For example, the Division of Measurement and Evaluation notifies instructors when it is time to create and release midterm evaluation forms, and students are initially notified and later reminded to fill out the forms. Finally, instructors are notified when the evaluation results are available online.

Instructors can choose both forced-choice and open-ended items from the existing EON item bank for their midterm evaluation forms. The item bank currently contains about two hundred questions that were either borrowed from the ICES item bank or developed with input from various EON stakeholders. Instructors can also write their own open-ended items for inclusion on their midterm evaluations.

Midterm evaluations are available to students during a two-week period. Results of the students' responses are summarized and made available to faculty immediately after the two-week period ends. This immediate access of results contributes to the success of the EON system.

Expanding Usage of the EON System. The first EON system pilot began in the summer 2001 term. Eleven instructors—mostly from the Online Graduate Library and Information Science program—participated in the first EON pilot; however, none used the midterm component. Since that first pilot, usage of the EON system has steadily increased, as has the use of EON's midterm evaluation component. In summer 2001, eleven courses used EON; in fall 2001, thirty-four; in spring 2002, thirty-nine; in summer 2002, seventeen; and in fall 2002, thirty-eight. The midterm component was used only in fall 2001 ($n = 5$), spring 2002 ($n = 3$), and fall 2002

($n = 10$). Note that summer terms offer fewer courses, and consequently EON summer usage is lower than during fall or spring.

Designing the Study   Research questions for this study were developed through the collaboration of the EON faculty advisory group and other colleagues. The purpose of the study was to gain a better understanding of how and why instructors use the midterm evaluation component and their general perceptions of the midterm component. The following questions guided the data collection efforts:

What are the instructors' perceptions of the various features and components of the EON midterm evaluation system?

Do instructors perceive differences in the way they developed the questions and used the results because the collection occurred online? Are there any perceived differences in the manner or type of responses given to these questions by the students?

What issues should be considered with an evolving online midterm evaluation system?

Defining the Participants and Developing the Questionnaire. Defining the participants was the easiest part of this study; participants were instructors who had used the midterm component of the EON system. Once the participants were identified, the interview protocol was developed. The protocol was based on the three general research questions given above and on the literature review. Then, approval was sought and granted from the university's Institutional Research Board.

During September 2002, the thirty-eight instructors using the EON system for their fall 2002 courses were contacted and asked if they planned to use EON to collect midterm student feedback. Those who responded affirmatively were invited to participate in the study. In addition, instructors who had used the EON midterm component in previous semesters were invited to participate in the study. From this pool, fourteen instructors were able and willing to be interviewed.

Conducting the Interviews and Summarizing the Responses. Participants were sent the interview questions a week in advance of the interviews. Most of the interviews were conducted face to face; however, three were conducted by telephone. The interviews averaged about an hour in length.

After the interviews were completed, each was summarized and categorized. The interview protocol provided a systematic approach to looking at the responses and considering them in light of both the research questions and the findings from the literature review.

Results

The interview results are reported below.

What are the instructors' perceptions of the various features and components of the EON mid-term evaluation system? To answer this question, instructors were asked for their perceptions about ease of use and problems that they experienced themselves or that their students reported to them. Two of the instructors reported that some of their students had trouble accessing the system to complete the midterm evaluation. This occurred because these students did not know their unique identification number or password required to access the system. This is a significant and recurring problem for UIUC online students in certain programs because they are given course-specific identifiers but do not realize that they also need to use their university identification number and password to access the system. This problem suggests the need for possible future training on the use of EON for both students and instructors.

All of the interviewees thought the system was at least fairly easy to maneuver and that its features were user friendly. Some users made suggestions to increase EON's usefulness. For example, one instructor indicated that he would like electronic notification when the evaluation forms had been sent to the students. This request was easily filled; the feature was simply added to the EON system.

Several interviewees mentioned issues associated with EON's item bank. At the time of the study, there was no separate item bank specifically for midterm evaluation forms. All forms (both end-of-term and midterm) had the same item bank of questions. Some interviewees noted that the questions were phrased in the past tense; this was problematic for use on a midterm evaluation. In addition, the instructors wanted more flexibility to design their own forced-choice items for midterm evaluations. Although EON allows instructors to write open-ended items, the system currently has no mechanism for instructors to design their own forced-choice items. Because of psychometric concerns about individually authored, forced-choice items, the issue of offering this option is still under consideration.

Do instructors perceive differences in the way they developed the questions and used the results because the collection occurred online? Are there any perceived differences in the type of responses given by students? All of the interviewees had used traditional paper-pencil feedback forms and thus could compare their perceptions of the online system with its paper-pencil counterpart. Interviewees reported feeling somewhat freer to add items to the survey because of the ease of modifying the instrument online. For example, nine instructors said they added more items on the EON forms than they had in the past on paper-pencil midterm forms.

Sometimes adding items to student evaluation surveys raises concerns that more items will reduce the substantive nature of the students' responses (some instructors assume, for example, that students may get tired and hurry through the remaining questions). But EON evaluations begin with fewer items than traditional end-of-term forms. Because the midterm survey initially has fewer items, increasing the number of items did not seem to have a negative effect on student responses.

Interviewees were also asked to comment about online versus paper-pencil response rates, but these comparisons were often like comparing apples and oranges. For example, some participants compared the response rate of online evaluations with that of paper-pencil midterm forms that were mailed to students in online classes. In these cases, EON had a higher response rate. Others compared EON with midterm paper-pencil forms administered to students in their on-campus classrooms. In these cases, the paper-pencil forms typically had a higher response rate.

When interviewees were asked about the number and intensity of negative student responses, results were mixed. Five interviewees said that EON responses were more negative. Four felt they were less negative, and the remainder noted no difference. In addition, the interviewees reported no problems with students' perceptions of confidentiality with regard to their online responses.

Eight of the fourteen interviewees reported that the online format lent itself to reading and summarizing responses more easily than did the paper-pencil format. The remainder were either unsure or had small enough classes that reading through handwritten comments had never been a problem.

What issues should be considered with an evolving online midterm evaluation system? For this question, interviewers asked instructors what support would be helpful and what suggestions they had to improve the EON midterm component. Responses regarding support fell into two categories: technical support and faculty development needs. Respondents who needed technical support wanted quick access to answers about technical questions for themselves and their students. In response, the Division of Measurement and Evaluation modified the EON Web site to include frequently asked questions and a more clearly identified path for technical support.

Several of the interviewees requested consultations on developing useful midterm feedback questions. They also wanted to more fully understand, and have a better context for, the student responses they receive. This is consistent with Seldin's (1999) finding that faculty development consultations are critical in helping instructors use feedback to improve their teaching. The division forwarded this information to the campus faculty development unit.

Summary and Conclusions

The EON system for collecting online student feedback is new at UIUC. With continued development and improvement of the new system come the promise of more flexibility and ease of access for both faculty and students. This study includes data from current and past users of EON's midterm feedback component. Fourteen faculty users were interviewed to provide information on three research questions.

In general, instructors reported that collecting midterm feedback online with the EON system was convenient. They requested more specific completion notifications for various steps in the process. In addition, they wanted access to items specifically designed for midterm evaluations. In comparing paper-pencil and online evaluation, instructors reported writing more questions and summarizing more quickly the student responses using the online system. They also reported that their students probably wrote more on their online evaluation forms than they did on paper-pencil forms. There was no consensus in regard to whether student responses submitted online were more or less negative than those submitted on paper-pencil forms.

The results of this study help validate the midterm component of EON. As the EON system is expanded and promoted, the division will highlight consultative services for item development and for the interpretation of results.

Implications for Future Research

As online midterm evaluation systems proliferate, the need to better understand technical support and faculty development will multiply. Although this study provides solid information about the needs of one campus, larger multi-institutional studies are clearly needed. Beyond the need for more generalizable studies lie specific areas of interest that also should be addressed by further research, including the design of effective evaluation items, timing for administering evaluations, and the use of survey results to improve teaching and learning. Furthermore, studies are needed on response rates for online midterm student feedback and on increasing the usefulness of results from these evaluations.

In addition, individual campuses must assess instructor and student accessibility to online resources. Although the World Wide Web Consortium has clear guidelines for accessibility compliance, thinking in terms of minimal standards is not enough. Access to information is a fundamental principle of higher education for all members of a learning community, and this accessibility must be extended to all the systems that are designed to collect course and instructor feedback online (Bar and Galuzzo, 1999). As technology gains an even greater foothold on college campuses, online evaluation systems such as EON will be further developed to better meet the needs of individuals and institutions of higher education.

References

Angelo, T. A., and Cross, K. P. *Classroom Assessment Techniques: A Handbook for College Teachers.* San Francisco: Jossey-Bass, 1994.

Ballantyne, C. "Why Survey Online? A Practical Look at Issues in the Use of the Internet for Surveys in Higher Education." Paper presented at the annual conference of the American Evaluation Association, Honolulu, Nov. 2000.

Bar, L., and Galuzzo, J. *The Accessible School: Universal Design for Educational Settings.* Berkeley, Calif.: MIG Communications, 1999.

Kulik, J. "Student Ratings: Validity, Utility, and Controversy." In Theall, M., Abrami, P., and Mets, L. (eds.), *The Student Ratings Debate: Are They Valid? How Can We Best Use Them?* New Directions for Institutional Research, no. 109. San Francisco: Jossey-Bass, 2001, pp. 9–25.

Overall, J. U., and Marsh, H. W. "Midterm Feedback from Students: Its Relationship to Instructional Improvement and Students' Cognitive and Affective Outcomes." *Journal of Educational Psychology,* 1979, 71(6), 856–865.

Scriven, M. "The Methodology of Evaluation." In R. W. Tyler, R. M. Gagné, and M. Scriven (eds.), *Perspectives of Curriculum Evaluation.* Chicago: Rand McNally, 1967, pp. 39–83.

Seldin, P. *Changing Practices in Evaluating Teaching: A Practical Guide to Improved Faculty Performance and Promotion.* Boston: Anker, 1999.

Sheehan, K. B. "E-mail Survey Response Rates: A Review." *Journal of Computer Mediated Communication,* 2001, 6(2). [http://www.ascusc.org/jcmc/vol6/issue2/sheehan.html]. Access date: Aug. 27, 2003.

CHERYL DAVIS BULLOCK is head of the Division of Measurement and Evaluation at the University of Illinois at Urbana-Champaign.

As the World Wide Web becomes an integral part of higher education, universities must determine the viability of using the Internet for their student evaluation systems. This chapter highlights important online-student-rating issues raised in this volume and in other research.

Online Evaluations of Teaching: An Examination of Current Practice and Considerations for the Future

Christina Ballantyne

Over the past fifty years, the world has seen huge changes in the use of technology. In many ways, higher education has been in the forefront of these changes. The development of the Internet over the past ten years, in particular, has resulted in new challenges for education. As universities and colleges move toward flexible modes of study, students have access to education whenever and wherever they choose.

Student evaluations of teaching have also experienced this technological shift. The move to online student surveys is currently an issue for many institutions. At Murdoch University in Perth, Western Australia, online evaluations of teaching have been used in targeted areas for four years. This chapter examines the Murdoch experience and reviews the experiences of other universities discussed in this volume.

Looking toward the future, Murdoch University, like many other institutions in the current global education marketplace, is moving toward a flexible learning environment where students select how and when they study. This introduces new challenges for the evaluation of teaching and courses. When there is no requirement for students to come to classes, the "captive audience" is lost. Is setting up an online evaluation system the way forward? If so, how do universities ensure that students respond? On the other hand, if the learning environment is to be truly flexible, evaluations also need to be flexible. Students, therefore, should have the opportunity to respond in class or online, a situation that may introduce new problems (for example, multiple response modes increase the possibility of duplicate responses or at least the perception by teachers that there may be duplication). This chapter discusses the future of teacher evaluation in the new flexible learning environment and promotes the view that online evaluation, like any evaluation, needs to be supported by individual instructors for it to work for the benefit of both teachers and students.

Background

The development of the Internet and computer technology has encouraged universities worldwide to adapt their courses in ways that enable them to make use of the technology. This shift has been influenced by a number of factors, including meeting the needs of a more diverse student population, confronting financial pressures on institutions (for example, the push to do more with less), and ensuring that graduates possess the technological skills increasingly needed for the workforce. In addition, most universities want to be at the cutting edge in many areas of practice, including the use of technology in their own operations.

Over the past ten years, student evaluations of teaching and courses have—at least in Australia—significantly increased, mainly due to a greater focus on the quality of teaching and the need for accountability. This focus on quality teaching has resulted in more formative evaluation for the purpose of improving teaching and learning (for example, classroom assessment techniques, midcourse evaluation, student focus groups). The focus on accountability has also resulted in more summative evaluation for promotion, teaching awards, funding decisions, and so forth. The convergence of these movements—technology and teaching improvement and accountability—has spurred the development of online student ratings of instruction.

Online Surveys of Courses at Murdoch University

Founded in 1975, Murdoch University is a small public institution (twelve thousand students) situated in Perth, Western Australia. The student population is somewhat nontraditional, with less than half of the undergraduate students coming to the university directly from high school; around one-quarter are studying part-time. About sixteen hundred students study entirely through distance-education classes, and another twelve hundred receive at least some part of their education through distance learning. In addition, overseas students, mostly from southeast Asia, constitute about 15 percent of the student population. Within the university, there are four divisions, each consisting of a number of schools. The university offers courses in the arts, business, education, engineering, law, science, and veterinary studies.

At Murdoch, mandatory evaluations of courses with standard questionnaires were introduced in 1994. Before this time, a voluntary, customized, "on-request" paper system was used. At present, 50 percent of the courses are surveyed each year, provided there are more than ten students enrolled in a course. The same applies for distance-education students. As is the case with most institutions, these student surveys are generally administered near the end of the semester as in-class paper questionnaires. The results of the course surveys are made available to deans of divisions, heads of schools, and course coordinators (faculty members who are responsible for the design and organization of the courses and, in most cases, for most of the teaching). Aggregated results for each division are posted on Murdoch University's Web site. In addition, faculty can receive feedback on their teaching through a "Student Survey of Teaching." These questionnaires are administered to instructors upon request, with the strong recommendation that they be distributed midsemester. Teachers who make use of this option then have the opportunity to respond to student concerns before the end of the semester. Student survey data are used in the calculation of the university's performance indicators and in making personnel and management decisions. Online evaluations have been introduced at Murdoch University as a gradual process, with the view that ultimately all surveys will move to online administration.

School of Engineering Pilot. In 1999, the university introduced online surveys of courses to the School of Engineering. This school was chosen for the pilot study of the online system for a number of reasons (Cummings and Ballantyne, 1999). First, the students in this school have a high level of computer literacy. Second, the school was one of the first at the university to introduce online components into its courses, and facilities were provided to give students twenty-four-hour access to computers. In addition, faculty in this school (and in particular the dean) were enthusiastic about adapting the paper student surveys to the Internet. Despite these favorable factors, the courses surveyed within the School of Engineering achieved an average response rate of only 30 percent for both semesters of 1999. In comparison, the previous paper forms had obtained a response rate of 65 percent. Yet, despite the low response rate, faculty and students were in favor of continuing with online surveys.

Based on faculty and student interest, the School of Engineering decided to proceed with the online student evaluations, and they used a variety of tactics to boost response rates: teachers making a concerted effort to promote the online survey, faculty providing students with information on the use of their feedback, and entering student participants in a drawing for a cash prize. With these strategies in place, response rates rose to 54 percent in the first semester of 2000 and 72 percent in the second semester. Unfortunately, this upsurge did not continue in 2001 and 2002, when response rates were around 50 percent.

Distance-Education Online Surveys. In the second semester of 2000, the university extended the use of the online survey system to distance-education students, who had previously been surveyed by mail only. All students were invited to complete the online surveys; students were sent a paper form only if they failed to complete the online survey by a specific date. In the first semester, only 14 percent of submissions were made online. In an effort to increase participation, administrators widened access to the student record system by issuing e-mail addresses to all students and adopting electronic transmission as the default mode of communication between students and the university. This improved communication meant that since 2001, students have been informed of the evaluation by e-mail with a hyperlink to the questionnaire. With these improvements to the system, the student response rate increased to 53 percent in 2001 and to 62 percent in 2002.

School of Information Technology Online Surveys. The School of Information Technology was the next group to initiate online surveys. This school seemed like a good candidate for online evaluation because the students have a high degree of computer literacy, and at the end of the semester when surveys are administered, these students are often working on independent projects away from the classroom. Hence, they are not together in one place to complete paper surveys. In 2001, the response rate for the in-class paper survey was only 40 percent. When online surveys were initiated in 2002, administrators were disappointed to find that the response rate remained at about 40 percent. However, the university has continued to move forward with online ratings, and several other university courses are now using the online system. Response rates in these courses vary widely (between 30 and 95 percent).

Issues Related to Online Surveys

From the research and experience of the authors contributing to this volume and from others who have written on the subject, a number of issues emerge regarding online evaluation: response rates; anonymity, confidentiality, and authentication; differences between online and paper survey results; and comparisons of costs.

Response Rates. Response rates concern all those who undertake survey research because good response rates help ensure the reliability of the data. Much of the current literature on online evaluation addresses the issue of lower response rates when converting to an online evaluation system (Cody, 1999; Dommeyer, Baum, and Hanna, 2002; Hmieleski, 2000; Hmieleski and Champagne, 2000). It appears that the fear of low response rates may be something that prevents some institutions from adopting an online evaluation system; some teachers have a perception that online ratings will result in lower response rates even before a system is implemented.

When Murdoch University implemented its online system, response rates for online ratings were initially low but later rose somewhat. Discussions with colleagues at other institutions in Australia revealed a comparable phenomenon at their institutions. Johnson (see Chapter Five) reports a similar experience with online response rates. Although there has been an increase in response rates at some universities, some institutions still struggle to achieve an adequate response rate. At Murdoch University, as mentioned above, several strategies have been effective in increasing response rates.

For any online system to work, students must have sufficient access to the Internet and to computing facilities. At Murdoch, courses were selected for online evaluation that already had considerable online components and in which students presumably had adequate access to the Internet. In addition, distance-education students were more easily contacted when complete e-mail address lists became available. As communication with these students improved, online rating submissions increased. In this volume, Bothell and Henderson (Chapter Seven) and Johnson (Chapter Five) comment on a similar situation at Brigham Young University (BYU) where an online rating system became more feasible once faculty and students had increased Internet access.

At Murdoch, another essential factor for good response rates is faculty support for the system, including making sure instructors communicate this support to their students. Research at Murdoch and at other institutions has shown that responding to students about changes made as a result of their feedback has positive effects (Ballantyne, 1999; Marlin, 1987; Migotsky, 2000; Spencer and Schmelkin, 2002). This communication to students not only makes them more likely to complete a feedback questionnaire, it also helps them feel that they are heard and that their concerns are considered.

In their study, Goodman and Campbell (1999) point out the importance of faculty support for an online rating system. Their research shows that response rates were high in the first semester of implementation, when faculty actively promoted the online system. However, response rates dropped when faculty support waned in the second semester. In other studies in this volume dealing with formative feedback, Bullock (Chapter Nine) and Tucker, Jones, Straker, and Cole (Chapter Eight) stress the benefits to teachers of immediately receiving evaluation results, a benefit that allows them to make changes within the current semester. Johnson's interviews with students support this finding; students want to know that their opinions are heard and that their feedback is acted on (Chapter Five). This closing of the feedback loop is easier in an online environment in which data can be quickly analyzed; then, faculty responses to the results can be quickly communicated to students by e-mail or a Web site.

Do incentives work in raising student response rates? Participating students in the School of Engineering at Murdoch were entered in a cash prize drawing for Aus.$100. Students were eligible to enter the drawing when they completed surveys for all courses in which they were enrolled. In addition, faculty support was enlisted, and students were told how their feedback was used to improve teaching. These efforts resulted in increased response rates. Johnson (Chapter Five) reports that BYU students supported the idea of incentives to increase response rates, particularly the early access to grades for those who rate their courses. He also found that teachers who gave extra credit for completion of the ratings received the best response rates. However, the issue of assigning extra credit is a difficult one. Is it legal or ethical? In Australia, for example, withholding access to grades would be considered particularly authoritative (Cummings and Ballantyne, 1999), and assigning extra credit would be unlikely to meet with student or institutional approval.

Anonymity, Confidentiality, and Authentication. When students complete evaluations of teaching, they need to be assured that they cannot be identified; paper forms traditionally do not ask for any identifying information. In addition, faculty need to be assured that only those students enrolled in the class complete the evaluations and that each student completes only one form. Although these requirements are relatively easy to achieve in a classroom setting, they require additional safeguards when collecting data online. These online safeguards require that students' identification be authenticated and protected. At Murdoch University, no authentication system has been developed yet. Students are asked to enter their student numbers, but their responses are accepted without them. (Currently, less than 5 percent of responses have no student numbers.) However, as the Murdoch system expands, the need for password protection becomes more apparent; in some cases, students submit multiple entries because they reconsider what they have said, they forget they have responded, or they simply hit the "Submit" button twice when the system is slow. As an online rating system is designed, safeguards for authentication and confidentiality can be built into the system, as they have been at Georgia Institute of Technology, BYU, and other institutions.

Differences Between Online and Paper Survey Results. Will online evaluations produce results different from those of paper evaluations? Given that evaluation results are often used for promotion and tenure decisions, online rating systems must provide information that is both valid and reliable. Much has been researched and written about the validity and reliability of paper ratings of instruction, but little has been researched or written in this regard about online ratings of instruction. Can we assume that the same properties exist for online evaluations as exist for paper evaluations? At Murdoch, no tests have been undertaken to investigate any psychometric differences in the responses because the courses evaluated online have been different from those evaluated on paper. For example, many of the Murdoch courses evaluated online are distance-education courses, with numbers too small to establish credible reliability. However, it may be that the differences are small. In this volume, Hardy (Chapter Three) reports little or no overall differences in online and paper evaluations. Johnson found a high correlation between the two modes on global teacher and course items.

In a University of Washington study, McGhee and Lowell (Chapter Four) researched online evaluations in a Web-based learning environment and compared these online evaluations with paper-based ratings in traditional classes. They concluded that differences in ratings are not likely due to whether students responded online or on paper; rather, these researchers suggest that any differences observed were likely due to differences in the environment and the types of students in online and on-campus classes. Likewise, Carini, Hayek, Kuh, and Ouimet (2003) found no systematic differences between paper and online evaluation results.

Concerning summary comments, some Murdoch teachers have reported that the comments students make on the Web-based evaluations differ from those on the paper evaluations. Students tend to make longer, more thoughtful comments on the Web. This finding is echoed by Bullock, Johnson, Tucker, and others in this volume.

Comparisons of Costs. Cost is an important consideration for institutions of higher education. Many educators assume that online evaluations are less costly because they eliminate the need for consumable paper forms and staff time to dispatch and process the paper forms. Bothell and Henderson (Chapter Seven) explore costs comparisons of online and paper rating systems. Based on their costs comparisons, they conclude that online student rating systems are considerably less expensive. Nevertheless, these authors point out the need for studies of cost-effectiveness of the two systems; future research is needed in this area.

The Future

What does the future hold for online evaluation? Students at Murdoch and at many other institutions enroll online, access their grades online, receive communications from the university online, and increasingly, have online components in their courses. It seems safe to predict that the use of online ratings of teaching is likely to increase in the future.

Murdoch University is currently pursuing a policy of introducing a flexible learning environment, with all courses converting to a "flexible" mode by 2007. Flexible learning means that students may access the course from the Web when and where they wish; there is no need for them to come to classes because the course material is provided online, including downloadable lectures that they can access on their own time. This blurring of the distinction between on-campus and distance-education students introduces a new challenge for collecting feedback from students. If students are able to study both online and in class, they should theoretically also be able to evaluate their classes either online or in the classroom. To do so, these "flexible-learning" students would need to provide identification for their rating forms (whether online or paper) to ensure no duplication—deliberate or accidental—occurs. At Murdoch and elsewhere, students seem confident that identifying information will be removed from their online evaluations. However, it is unlikely that students would feel confident that their anonymity would be protected if they identified themselves on the paper forms. This protection is necessary because at Murdoch and other universities, paper forms are sent to teachers so that they can read the student comments. If students were identified on the paper forms, teachers would know which students made the comments. (This could be resolved by typing or photocopying students' comments, but at Murdoch, and often at other universities, there are not sufficient resources available for these activities.) The students' confidentiality is only one of the concerns that arise from efforts to provide both online and paper evaluations for the same course.

Five courses used the flexible-learning model at Murdoch during the second semester of 2002, and an evaluation was carried out using an online survey; students who did not complete the online survey were mailed a paper survey. This is an expensive solution that could not be sustained if all courses became flexible. For reasons of confidentiality and cost, an online-only system appears to be the best option as more courses convert to the flexible model.

Low response rates, whether actual or perceived, seem to be hampering the adoption of online evaluation systems. Johnson states, "At BYU, response rates are the primary concern about online student ratings of instruction" (Chapter Five). On the other hand, some high response rates have been reported in this volume for individual campuses and individual courses; by using appropriate strategies, it *is* possible to obtain good response rates.

Hardy (Chapter Three) poses a related question about online response rates:"Which is more valid. . . . evaluations from a greater number of students (some of whom will enter almost anything just to have it finished and leave class) or collecting evaluations from fewer students who have definite ideas concerning the class?" Hardy raises an important issue: the views of students who have something to say are often more useful than perfunctory responses from disinterested students. However, when these data are used for summative purposes, can decisions be based on a limited sample of student responses? What level of response is acceptable to the stakeholders in the evaluation process?

Conclusion

The authors of this volume have identified a number of benefits of online rating systems: lower costs; more class time for teaching (instead of completing paper rating forms in class); ease of administration; more flexible design options; greater accessibility for students; more complete data collection; longer, more thoughtful student comments; reduced turnaround time; more accurate data collection and reporting; reduced staff time for processing; more detailed, user-friendly reports; and greater ease in responding to students in order to close the feedback loop. Given the benefits of online rating systems, can we cope with their possible deficits in areas such as response rates, development costs, response bias, and confidentiality and anonymity issues?

Some research has addressed these possible deficits. For example, Johnson (Chapter Five) and Thorpe (2002) found no response-rate bias in their studies of online ratings. Johnson and other researchers also suggest that appropriate strategies can raise response rates of online student ratings (for example, enlisting faculty support for the online evaluation system and communicating to students how their feedback is used). As more research is conducted in these and other areas, institutions will be better equipped to consider effective evaluation systems and how they can be used to improve teaching and learning.

References

Ballantyne, C. "Improving University Teaching: Responding to Feedback from Students." In Zepke, N., Knight, M., Leach, L., and Viskovic, A. (eds.), *Adult Learning Cultures: Challenges and Choices in Times of Change.* Wellington, Australia: WP Press, 1999.

Carini, R. M., Hayek, J. C., Kuh, G. D., and Ouimet, J. A. "College Student Responses to Web and Paper Surveys: Does Mode Matter?" *Research in Higher Education,* 2003, 44(1), 1–19. [http://www.kluweronline.com/issn/0361–0365/contents]. Access date: July 14, 2003.

Cody, A. "Evaluation Via the Web." *Teaching and Education News,* 1999, 9(6). University of Queensland. [http://www.tedi.uq.edu.au/TEN/TEN_previous/TEN4_99/index.html]. Access date: Aug. 27, 2003.

Cummings, R., and Ballantyne, C. "Student Feedback on Teaching: Online! On Target?" *Evaluation: Challenging Boundaries.* Proceedings of the Annual International Conference of the Australasian Evaluation Society, Perth, Oct. 1999.

Dommeyer, C. J., Baum, P., and Hanna, R. W. "College Students' Attitudes Towards Methods of Collecting Teaching Evaluations: In-Class Versus on-Line." *Journal of Education for Business,* 2002, 78(1), 11–15.

Goodman, A., and Campbell, M. "Developing Appropriate Administrative Support for Online Teaching with an Online Course Evaluation System." 1999. [http://www.deakin.edu.au/~agoodman/publications/isimade99.php]. Access date: Apr. 19, 2003.

Hmieleski, K. "Barriers to Online Evaluation: Surveying the Nation's Top 200 Most Wired Colleges." Troy, N.Y.: Interactive and Distance Education Assessment (IDEA) Laboratory, Rensselaer Polytechnic Institute, 2000 (Unpublished report).

Hmieleski, K., and Champagne, M. "Plugging into Course Evaluation." *Technology Source,* Sept./Oct. 2000. [http://ts.mivu.org/dfault.asp?show=articleandid=795]. Access date: Apr. 22, 2003.

Marlin, J. W. Jr. "Student Perception of End of Course Evaluations." *Journal of Higher Education,* 1987, 58, 704–716.

Migotsky, C. P. "Student Perceptions of Student Ratings: Construct Validity Revisited." Paper presented at the annual conference of the American Evaluation Association, Honolulu, Nov. 2000.

Spencer, K. J. and Schmelkin, L. P. "Student Perspectives on Teaching and Its Evaluation." *Assessment and Evaluation in Higher Education,* 2002, 27(5), 397–409.

Thorpe, S. W. "Online Student Evaluation of Instruction: An Investigation of Non-Response Bias." Paper presented at the 42nd Annual Forum for Institutional Research, Toronto, June 2002. [http://www.drexel.edu/provost/ir/conf/bias.pdf]. Access date: July 13, 2003.

CHRISTINA BALLANTYNE is a project officer in the Teaching and Learning Centre at Murdoch University in Perth, Western Australia, where she is responsible for the student evaluation system throughout the university.

Index

UIUC (University of Illinois at Urbana-Champaign): EON (Evaluation ONLine) feedback system of, 95–101; increase of online courses at, 95

UW (University of Washington) course ratings, 40

Versatility issue, 77

Wall, T. D., 89

Warr, P., 89

Waschull, S. B., 39, 47

Web sites: Australian CEQ (Course Experience Questionnaire), 83; IDEA

Center, 11; of institutions using online student ratings, 22–24; Murdoch University, 105; Online Student Evaluation of Teaching (OnSET), 2, 18

Weimer, M., 13, 81, 89

Whetten, D. A., 12, 13, 14, 15

Wisher, R. A., 70

WSU College of Veterinary Medicine survey, 76–77

WSU (Washington State University): data on costs gathered at, 69; personnel time expended in processing paper-based surveys, 76–77

Yale University, 17, 77

Back Issue/Subscription Order Form

Copy or detach and send to:

Jossey-Bass, A Wiley Company, 989 Market Street, San Francisco CA 94103-1741

Call or fax toll-free: Phone 888-378-2537 6:30AM – 3PM PST; Fax 888-481-2665

Back Issues: Please send me the following issues at $27 each
(Important: please include ISBN number with your order.)

_____

_____

_____

$ _____   Total for single issues

$ _____   SHIPPING CHARGES: SURFACE   Domestic Canadian

		Domestic	Canadian
	First Item	$5.00	$6.00
	Each Add'l Item	$3.00	$1.50

For next-day and second-day delivery rates, call the number listed above.

Subscriptions   Please __ start __ renew my subscription to *New Directions for Teaching and Learning* for the year 2___at the following rate:

U.S.	__ Individual $80		__ Institutional $160
Canada	__ Individual $80		__ Institutional $200
All Others	__ Individual $104		__ Institutional $234
Online Subscription			__ Institutional $145

**For more information about online subscriptions visit
www.interscience.wiley.com**

$ _____   Total single issues and subscriptions (Add appropriate sales tax for your state for single issue orders. No sales tax for U.S. subscriptions. Canadian residents, add GST for subscriptions and single issues.)

__Payment enclosed (U.S. check or money order only)
__VISA __ MC __ AmEx __ #_____ Exp. Date _____

Signature _____ Day Phone _____
__ Bill Me (U.S. institutional orders only. Purchase order required.)

Purchase order # _____
                Federal Tax ID13559302   GST 89102 8052

Name _____

Address _____

_____

Phone _____ E-mail _____

For more information about Jossey-Bass, visit our Web site at www.josseybass.com

OTHER TITLES AVAILABLE IN THE
NEW DIRECTIONS FOR TEACHING AND LEARNING SERIES
Marilla D. Svinicki, Editor-in-Chief
R. Eugene Rice, Consulting Editor

TL95   **Problem-Based Learning in the Information Age**
Dave S. Knowlton, David C. Sharp
Provides information about theories and practices associated with problem-based learning, a pedagogy that allows students to become more engaged in their own education by actively interpreting information. Today's professors are adopting problem-based learning across all disciplines to faciliate a broader, modern definition of what it means to learn. Authors provide practical experience about designing useful problems, creating conducive learning environments, facilitating students' activities, and assessesing students' efforts at problem solving.
ISBN: 0-7879-7172-3

TL94   **Technology: Taking the Distance out of Learning**
Margit Misangyi Watts
This volume addresses the possibilities and challenges of computer technology in higher education. The contributors examine the pressures to use technology, the reasons not to, the benefits of it, the feeling of being a learner as well as a teacher, the role of distance education, and the place of computers in the modern world. Rather than discussing only specific successes or failures, this issue addresses computers as a new cultural symbol and begins meaningful conversations about technology in general and how it affects education in particular.
ISBN: 0-7879-6989-3

TL93   **Valuing and Supporting Undergraduate Research**
Joyce Kinkead
The authors gathered in this volume share a deep belief in the value of undergraduate research. Research helps students develop skills in problem solving, critical thinking, and communication, and undergraduate researchers' work can contribute to institution's quest to further knowledge and help meet societal challenges. Chapters provide an overview of undergraduate research, explore programs at different types of institutions, and offer suggestions on how faculty members can find ways to work with undergraduate researchers.
ISBN: 0-7879-6907-9

TL92   **The Importance of Physical Space in Creating Supportive Learning Environments**
Nancy Van Note Chism, Deborah J. Bickford
The lack of extensive dialogue on the importance of learning spaces in higher education environments prompted the essays in this volume. Chapter authors look at the topic of learning spaces from a variety of perspectives, elaborating on the relationship between physical space and learning, arguing for an expanded notion of the concept of learning spaces and furnishings, talking about the context within which decision making for learning spaces takes place, and discussing promising approaches to the renovation of old learning spaces and the construction of new ones.
ISBN: 0-7879-6344-5

United States Postal Service

Statement of Ownership, Management, and Circulation

1. Publication Title	2. Publication Number	3. Filing Date
New Directions For Teaching & Learning	8 2 7 1 - 0 6 3 3	9/30/03

4. Issue Frequency	5. Number of Issues Published Annually	6. Annual Subscription Price
Quarterly	4	$80 Individual $160 Institution

7. Complete Mailing Address of Known Office of Publication (Not printer) (Street, city, county, state, and ZIP+4)

989 Market Street
San Francisco, CA 94103-1741

San Francisco County

Contact Person
Joe Schuman

Telephone
415 782 3232

8. Complete Mailing Address of Headquarters or General Business Office of Publisher (Not printer)

Same as above

9. Full Names and Complete Mailing Addresses of Publisher, Editor, and Managing Editor (Do not leave blank)

Publisher (Name and complete mailing address)

Wiley, San Francisco
Jossey-Bass - Pfeiffer
Address - same as above

Editor (Name and complete mailing address)

Marilla D. Svinicki
Cntr For Teaching Effectiveness/Univ. of Austin
Main Bldg. 2200
Austin TX 78712-1111

Managing Editor (Name and complete mailing address)

None

10. Owner (Do not leave blank. If the publication is owned by a corporation, give the name and address of the corporation immediately followed by the names and addresses of all stockholders owning or holding 1 percent or more of the total amount of stock. If not owned by a corporation, give the names and addresses of the individual owners. If owned by a partnership or other unincorporated firm, give its name and address as well as those of each individual owner. If the publication is published by a nonprofit organization, give its name and address.)

Full Name	Complete Mailing Address
John Wiley & Sons Inc.	111 River Street Hoboken, NJ 07030

11. Known Bondholders, Mortgagees, and Other Security Holders Owning or Holding 1 Percent or More of Total Amount of Bonds, Mortgages, or Other Securities. If none, check box ▶ ☐ None

Full Name	Complete Mailing Address
Same as above	Same as above

12. Tax Status (For completion by nonprofit organizations authorized to mail at nonprofit rates) (Check one)
The purpose, function, and nonprofit status of this organization and the exempt status for federal income tax purposes:
☐ Has Not Changed During Preceding 12 Months
☐ Has Changed During Preceding 12 Months (Publisher must submit explanation of change with this statement)

PS Form 3526, October 1999   (See Instructions on Reverse)

---

13. Publication Title	14. Issue Date for Circulation Data Below
New Directions For Teaching And Learning	Summer 2003

15. Extent and Nature of Circulation		Average No. Copies Each Issue During Preceding 12 Months	No. Copies of Single Issue Published Nearest to Filing Date
a. Total Number of Copies (Net press run)		1,618	1,682
b. Paid and/or Requested Circulation	(1) Paid/Requested Outside-County Mail Subscriptions Stated on Form 3541. (Include advertiser's proof and exchange copies)	937	948
	(2) Paid In-County Subscriptions Stated on Form 3541 (Include advertiser's proof and exchange copies)	0	0
	(3) Sales Through Dealers and Carriers, Street Vendors, Counter Sales, and Other Non-USPS Paid Distribution	0	0
	(4) Other Classes Mailed Through the USPS	0	0
c. Total Paid and/or Requested Circulation (Sum of 15b. (1), (2),(3),and (4)) ▶		937	948
d. Free Distribution by Mail (Samples, complimentary, and other free)	(1) Outside-County as Stated on Form 3541	0	0
	(2) In-County as Stated on Form 3541	0	0
	(3) Other Classes Mailed Through the USPS	2	2
e. Free Distribution Outside the Mail (Carriers or other means)		41	41
f. Total Free Distribution (Sum of 15d. and 15e.) ▶		43	43
g. Total Distribution (Sum of 15c. and 15f) ▶		980	991
h. Copies not Distributed		638	691
i. Total (Sum of 15g. and h.) ▶		1,618	1,682
j. Percent Paid and/or Requested Circulation (15c. divided by 15g. times 100)		96%	96%

16. Publication of Statement of Ownership
☐ Publication required. Will be printed in the Winter 2003 issue of this publication.   ☐ Publication not required.

17. Signature and Title of Editor, Publisher, Business Manager, or Owner

[signature]   Susan E. Lewis
VP & Publisher - Periodicals

Date 9/30/03

I certify that all information furnished on this form is true and complete. I understand that anyone who furnishes false or misleading information on this form or who omits material or information requested on the form may be subject to criminal sanctions (including fines and imprisonment) and/or civil sanctions (including civil penalties).

Instructions to Publishers

1. Complete and file one copy of this form with your postmaster annually on or before October 1. Keep a copy of the completed form for your records.

2. In cases where the stockholder or security holder is a trustee, include in items 10 and 11 the name of the person or corporation for whom the trustee is acting. Also include the names and addresses of individuals who are stockholders who own or hold 1 percent or more of the total amount of bonds, mortgages, or other securities of the publishing corporation. In item 11, if none, check the box. Use blank sheets if more space is required.

3. Be sure to furnish all circulation information called for in item 15. Free circulation must be shown in items 15d, e, and f.

4. Item 15h., Copies not Distributed, must include (1) newsstand copies originally stated on Form 3541, and returned to the publisher, (2) estimated returns from news agents, and (3), copies for office use, leftovers, spoiled, and all other copies not distributed.

5. If the publication had Periodicals authorization as a general or requester publication, this Statement of Ownership, Management, and Circulation must be published; it must be printed in any issue in October or, if the publication is not published during October, the first issue printed after October.

6. In item 16, indicate the date of the issue in which this Statement of Ownership will be published.

7. Item 17 must be signed.

(Failure to file or publish a statement of ownership may lead to suspension of Periodicals authorization.)

PS Form 3526, October 1999 (Reverse)

NEW DIRECTIONS FOR TEACHING AND LEARNING IS NOW AVAILABLE ONLINE AT WILEY INTERSCIENCE

What is Wiley InterScience?

Wiley InterScience is the dynamic online content service from John Wiley & Sons delivering the full text of over 300 leading scientific, technical, medical, and professional journals, plus major reference works, the acclaimed Current Protocols laboratory manuals, and even the full text of select Wiley print books online.

What are some special features of Wiley InterScience?

Wiley Interscience Alerts is a service that delivers table of contents via e-mail for any journal available on Wiley InterScience as soon as a new issue is published online.
EarlyView is Wiley's exclusive service presenting individual articles online as soon as they are ready, even before the release of the compiled print issue. These articles are complete, peer-reviewed, and citable.
CrossRef is the innovative multi-publisher reference linking system enabling readers to move seamlessly from a reference in a journal article to the cited publication, typically located on a different server and published by a different publisher.

How can I access Wiley InterScience?

Visit http://www.interscience.wiley.com.

Guest Users can browse Wiley InterScience for unrestricted access to journal tables of contents and article abstracts, or use the powerful search engine.
Registered Users are provided with a *Personal Home Page* to store and manage customized alerts, searches, and links to favorite journals and articles. Additionally, Registered Users can view free online sample issues and preview selected material from major reference works.
Licensed Customers are entitled to access full-text journal articles in PDF, with select journals also offering full-text HTML.

How do I become an Authorized User?

Authorized Users are individuals authorized by a paying Customer to have access to the journals in Wiley InterScience. For example, a university that subscribes to Wiley journals is considered to be the Customer.
Faculty, staff and students authorized by the university to have access to those journals in Wiley InterScience are Authorized Users. Users should contact their library for information on which Wiley journals they have access to in Wiley InterScience.

ASK YOUR INSTITUTION ABOUT WILEY INTERSCIENCE TODAY!